D.R. HEATH

ALEXANDER SALVADOR

AND THE DISCOVERY OF DETERMINATE

BOOK 1

This edition first published in paperback by
Michael Terence Publishing in 2023
www.mtp.agency

ISBN 9781800945173

Michael Terence
Publishing

***

"I don't know where I came from. I've been here for 200 years and no one around me seems to have noticed."

Every day as Determinate drove up and down the track, he took passengers on journeys to and from their chosen destinations. For some people, this was to and from work or school, whilst others were travelling to social outings, visiting the countryside or the big city. Determinate would do this journey, travelling from the countryside to the big city, and back again, several times a day, every month of the year, never getting bored! No two days aboard Determinate were the same. There was always some sort of problem for him to solve, it kept him pretty occupied, so the journeys never really got a chance to become tedious for him.

There was something very mysterious about Determinate. Unlike other trains, he could see, hear, smell, taste and feel things just like you and I. No one had ever noticed that the train they were on had all five senses. In fact, not only did no one know this about Determinate, but he had no explanation himself about *how* he was able to do these things.

He had tried to catch the attention of the other trains before, but none of them ever responded. At first, he thought that was because the humans were around, and they were being careful not to get caught.

Determinate had overheard the children whispering about awful sounding places called 'labs' - not to be confused with the four-legged passengers who sometimes boarded the train too - where "new" and confusing things such as advanced trains like Determinate could be taken apart and studied. Determinate wasn't very keen on the sound of that. It made sense that all the other trains felt the same way about avoiding that outcome at all costs too. He would hear them communicate daily when passing each other on the tracks, or at the train yard, using their central processing unit (CPU) system. He had been so sure that it meant that they could speak too, but at night when all the trains stopped working, the other trains still didn't speak. Determinate had realised, he wasn't like the other trains.

Having all five senses had its perks for Determinate, for example when he saw that there might be platform problems, he would look for a free platform and discreetly begin to prepare himself to smoothly switch tracks towards it before the controller had to give the instructions. There was a reason he was still the king of smooth transitions. There had been so many times over the years when Determinate's secret abilities helped to overcome challenges at work; avoiding collisions, derailments, navigating level crossings and even avoiding trespassing passengers on the train line. Every time something like that happened mysteriously, all the safety train controllers, engineers, local scholars and transport investigators were puzzled. How was this old train still chugging along? Why and how was it never involved in a serious incident?

No one seemed to notice the other unanswered questions such as the fact that no one was sure where Determinate came from, where, or *when* he was made; everyone just knew that Determinate had been there ever since they could remember. Even the older generations weren't sure when exactly he came there, it was just widely accepted that he had been there even before they were born. Determinate was actually a 200-year mystery, but even he didn't know that.

But being such a mystery meant that Determinate was starting to feel a little bit restless and dreamed of breaking centuries of silence. He really wanted to communicate with all the interesting people around, but the fear of being taken to those terrible 'labs' always held him back.

As Determinate travelled from village to village each day, transporting different types of commuters, he saw some of his regular passengers. Alvin was just one of them. He would catch the train at 8 am every morning without fail to arrive at work by 9 am every weekday. Then there was little Johnny and his family, who would always embark on their journey just as moody Mary disembarked with her friend, Alexander, a few stops later, some days. There were many other people that Determinate had noticed from their frequent travels, such as the school children from the nearby villages for example. Determinate really liked how diverse every passenger was, they all seemed to have their own quirky habits and subtly different behavioural patterns.

On one hand, although Determinate knew it was a little bit cheeky, overhearing everyone's gossip and secrets could be quite funny. On the other hand, this meant that he could also hear every criticism the passengers made about him. Some days they complained about his shape or design, on other days it was his speed, the sounds he made, or even that his seats were uncomfortable during their daily commute. It was becoming harder and harder for Determinate to hear each day, he so badly wanted to suggest ways to help improve his passengers' experiences, but he couldn't risk revealing himself.

Feeling all the emotions that you and I experience but being unable to do anything about it, left Determinate often feeling saddened. He had started noticing that on many occasions when he was feeling down, he had begun to physically slow down. He started thinking about how he had been very faithful, every day and night, serving all the same people who were complaining about him and criticising him. He had tried many different ways to find solutions to please all of his passengers, but if he sped up to make Hellen happy, Charlie would be holding his seat for dear life terrified of how quickly the outside world was passing by his window. Determinate came to the realisation that he would never be able to please everyone, every time, so all he could do was be the best he could, at all times. As his older and wiser passenger, Miss Anderson liked to remind her grandchildren *"one can only try their best"*.

Despite knowing that he couldn't possibly make everyone happy, Determinate couldn't shake the feeling of wanting to improve his services to give his passengers the best experience. The more the passengers criticised him, the more he felt absolutely determined to make it happen. Maybe there was a reason he was given the name Determinate? It didn't help that he was very observant with an equally great memory either; all the comments just kept accumulating in his memory making him want to finally break his silence more and more each day.

He felt like he had to speak to someone, but who could he choose? He would have to be very careful. Determinate thought to himself about who might be best to speak to. After a short while, it occurred to him that there were only a few people he could think of that he might be able to trust. There was Alvin whom Determinate had known for over 60 years, since Alvin's childhood, travelling on the trains with his family. Little Johnny whom he had known for over 9 years, moody Mary whom he had known for over 17 years and her friend, Alexander. People often remarked comically that they were like magpies. Perhaps Determinate could break his silence and confide in them, but how would he bring them together without scaring them away?

As Alvin was getting off the train one night, he heard his name, "Alvin, Alvin, Alvin," Determinate called, quietly in a very low voice.

Alvin paused mid-step. He was sure he was the last passenger to leave the train. He took everything a little slower these days so he could observe all the little things that others were too busy to notice. He looked from side to side and saw no one. He frowned wondering if he was hearing things. Shaking his head, he continued walking; maybe he did need an appointment for a hearing assessment, as his grandson had so cheekily suggested, after all.

But as Alvin continued to walk, he heard his name called again. Alvin was sure he had heard it this time, yet there was still no one else in sight. Goosebumps covered his arms and neck… What was that? Who was that? Was there a ghost?! Alvin hobbled as quickly as he could from the platform. He was sure he must have looked rather odd whilst making his great escape. However, he would have much preferred to continue looking odd than try to make friends with Casper the ghost at night.

The next morning, Determinate had decided to try reaching out to Johnny as he and his family were getting ready to board the train. However, just before he spoke, Determinate noticed that the platform was more crowded than usual. Looking around, he noted that there were lots of train inspectors, the local superintendent of police, as well as more passengers than there should have been after the first train would have left the station.

Cautiously, Determinate listened intently to overhear what the inspectors were speaking about, to see if he could get any clues about what was going on. He was shocked to discover that all of this commotion was caused by the fact that a train had gone missing. Again. That was the second time this year! Determinate wondered briefly if they had a train thief, but then he questioned how exactly a train could be stolen without anyone noticing, *even him*. That was impossible. But "*where did the trains go?*" he became curious. Determinate wasn't alone in his confusion, everyone was puzzled about the same questions, *who* was stealing the trains? And *how* were they doing it?

Determinate noticed little Johnny fighting his way through the crowd whilst holding his mother's hand to get on the train. In the nine years he had known him, Determinate thought Johnny was a courageous boy. It seemed Johnny wasn't afraid of anything. Determinate knew that Johnny would choose to sit at the front of the train; he always sat there. This time was no exception. He heard when Johnny, after sitting down, quietly said to himself that he wished the train seat was warmer. Maybe this was the best way to catch little Johnny's attention. Now was his chance to reach out to Johnny. A warmer seat coming right up!

Johnny shuffled around in his seat, was it his imagination or was the seat actually getting warmer? After a few minutes had passed, Johnny was sure that this was real. His seat had actually gotten warmer after he wished it. It was very weird. Johnny hadn't heard of anything like it happening before, so he jumped out of his seat to run to his mother, who was sitting a few seats back.

"Mum! Mum!" he shouted in astonishment. As soon as he reached her, he began excitedly telling her what had just happened. "I made a wish for the train seat to get warm, and it did, it did, Mummy!"

Johnny's Mum's eyebrows raised, and then she frowned replying, "Garbage, this train is too old for that kind of technology."

Johnny looked at his Mum incredulously as he protested, trying to tell her that it was true, but his Mum wasn't having any of it and told him sternly to stop being silly and to sit back down in his seat before the train began to move again. There was no way of convincing her.

Little Johnny trudged back to his seat, knowing that this experience was true and real. Maybe he needed to test his theory. After all, if it happened again, then his Mum *had* to believe him. Very quietly he said, "Dear wishing fairy, I am going to make another wish. I wish the train would slow down when we are passing the big colourful lake, so I can look at it longer." He sat quietly, eagerly waiting for the lake to come up to prove his suspicions right or wrong. Sure enough, as the lake appeared up ahead, the train began to slow all the way down and Johnny was able to really take in the view. Little Johnny was now convinced that someone or something was granting his wishes.

Johnny spent the whole of the train journey wondering how to make sense of the magical events that were happening. He had decided that it couldn't be a fairy because he hadn't seen any tiny people with wings flying around anywhere. He had been keeping an eye out for them the whole journey. Even when Johnny was getting off the train, he still hadn't found an answer. To Johnny, 'not a fairy,' was not a good enough answer to this great question.

Slightly disappointed, he stepped off of the train when he heard a voice whisper, "It was me who granted you all of those wishes."

Johnny's head darted from side to side trying to catch a glimpse of where this voice came from, but he didn't see anyone. He huffed, frustrated at having missed the magical moment again. The voice had been very calm, so although Johnny was surprised, he didn't feel afraid. He couldn't let this opportunity pass, he had to find out who, or what had spoken. Maybe if he spoke back to the voice, he could keep it speaking long enough to see where it was coming from.

"Can I call you a Genie, master, whoever you are?"

"It's me, Johnny, the train speaking," came the voice again.

The train?! A talking train? Johnny thought excitedly. Johnny's inquisitive nature started taking over. He had so many questions. He wanted to know more. He wanted to know *everything*. Little Johnny could hardly contain himself; the talking train even knew his name!

"Can you really talk? That's sooo, sooo, cool! No one would even believe me if I told them!"

Straightaway, Determinate responded alarmed, to a practically buzzing Johnny, "Oh no. No, please don't tell anyone about me. The engineers will take me away for testing because I'm so different from the others." Determinate was relieved to see the boy nod slightly in understanding.

"You're a unique train," Johnny whispered, as his Mum whisked him off to school. Johnny could hardly wait to finish school that day to get the same train back home. He would store up all his questions and ask the train on the way home. Johnny's most pressing question was, how could he hear the train so clearly when it seemed no one else had? It was puzzling.

Other people thought Mary seemed rude and unapproachable. It had gotten to the point where she had very few friends. Her best friend was Alexander. He was very clever, especially in computer programming. Everyone would call him a computer and technology wizard! To everyone else, Mary and Alexander looked like great friends, but Determinate was sure that he was picking up on some romance going on too. Years ago, she had been bullied by some of the other students in her school, Rainbow Secondary School. As a result, Mary didn't speak much anymore, she kept herself to herself, and didn't speak to anyone, especially on the train. The only time she would really speak was when Mary and magpie Alexander would sit together. Unsurprisingly, they sat together all the time. Determinate thought that Mary and Alexander would be perfect to confide in, but it could be challenging to get through to them.

One day, at her regular station, the Rainbow Station, Determinate noticed that Mary wasn't at her usual platform yet. He looked around and glimpsed her running toward her platform in a rush. She was running late, but Alexander was already on the train keeping her seat free with his rucksack. Determinate saw that as

Mary ran for the train, her purse fell from her pocket, hitting the wooden panelled decoration with a thud. Determinate was about to be running late himself, the departing whistles had already been sounded. Perhaps this was the perfect opportunity to make contact with Mary, he thought to himself, and alert her that she had dropped her purse. Then he would wait for her to get it and board the train.

"Mary, you have dropped your purse," said Determinate. "Go and get it, I'll wait for you."

Mary was very much confused, but patting her pockets, she found that they were indeed empty. Worried, she looked behind her, scanning the ground for her purse. Then she spotted it, along with a shiny coin. She quickly ran to retrieve the purse and the shiny coin, thinking that it must have fallen out of her purse, and finally boarding the train. Her heart was pounding; what a rush! She remembered that the voice had come from nearer the front of the train, where the platform conductor was standing, or perhaps by the window where Alexander was sitting.

When she went up to the conductor to thank him for his help, he looked confused and tilted his head to one side, asking what she was thanking him for. Mary's eyebrows scrunched together, as she explained the whole situation, but the train conductor seemed even more confused as if he had no idea what Mary was talking about. Mary reached her seat, wondering who had spoken to her. Since it was clearly not the conductor, it had to be Alexander calling from the window.

"Was it you calling from the window of the train telling me that I dropped my purse?"

"No, Mary," he replied. "All the windows are closed." She explained the whole situation again to him. "Maybe it was someone else?" said Alexander. She was then even more confused.

However, Mary had homework to be getting on with and didn't have time to waste thinking about who had spoken to her. As she was putting away the purse and the coin, she noticed something extremely unusual about it. This coin wasn't something she had ever seen before. The language and date were mysterious. Nevertheless, she put it away and took out her homework, to get an early start on it, as she always did. Alexander was on his laptop as always. Determinate knew that he had to do something to catch her attention. Mary was concentrating so hard to complete her homework and seemed to be struggling with the concept of Pythagoras' theorem. Determinate knew that Alexander could help, but Mary was too nervous to ask, therefore he knew this would be a perfect opportunity to reach out to her.

"Mary, hey Mary!" he whispered, trying to gain her attention.

Mary began looking around to see who was calling her, as she was sure the voice didn't belong to Alexander, who was sitting right beside her. Determinate noticed that although Mary had clearly heard him, and was looking around for the source of the voice, no one else had batted an eyelash. In fact, now that Determinate thought about it, every time he had spoken, no one apart from the person he was speaking to had budged. The other people *couldn't* hear him!

"Don't be afraid," said Determinate "it's the train, I can speak."

Mary's eyes opened wide, and her mouth hung slightly open. "Shut up! Shut up!" she demanded, shaking her head vigorously. Still in shock, she brought her hand to her temple. "I think I'm going crazy trying to understand this topic!" She paused before she whispered to herself exasperatedly, "Am I really hearing voices?"

Alexander, who had witnessed the entire situation, became very worried. Turning to face her, he asked calmly, "Mary, are you okay? You were talking to yourself, and you sounded like you were getting quite upset and agitated."

Mary slowly and gently rested her head on Alexander's shoulder. Initially, Alexander froze, tense with shock before relaxing. It was the first time Mary had ever done that. As Mary began to explain to him, what had just happened to her, and the strange voice she had heard calling her name. After Alexander had heard the whole story, she realised that he hadn't been *listening* at all; he was entirely distracted by these odd new sensations he was feeling for the first time in his life. He didn't quite know how to explain what was happening to him, he felt hot and cold simultaneously, which was nonsensical. *Everything* felt nonsensical. All he knew for sure was that, at this present moment, he felt like he was secure from all harm and danger; and that he was so light that he was certain he could glide through the universe without wings. He felt *immortal.* Alexander had gotten so overwhelmed with this feeling, that it had fully overtaken his awareness of what Mary was even saying to him. Despite being that close, Alexander still did not catch a single word that Mary had just said.

Meanwhile, the old lady who was headed to the market, sitting opposite Mary, had noticed Mary talking to herself too. The woman looked over her glasses concerned saying to Mary, "Oh no, lovely, it isn't good to be all stressed and talking to yourself like that at all. I think you should give that studying a break, love," she tutted.

Determinate almost chuckled as the two magpies cracked sheepish smiles, in response to the very direct, yet well-meaning, elderly stranger across from them. When the old lady went back to looking out of the window, and the two had stopped immaturely sniggering at Alvin's tongue-in-cheek comment, "Great, now she'll forever think you've lost your marbles," Determinate spoke again.

"Mary, you're the only one that can hear me. Well, apart from little Johnny, and Alvin of course, who are also my friends."

Mary's face scrunched up in disbelief. "What?! Shut. Up," she shouted in response. "Have you already spoken to them?"

Alexander who was getting really concerned all over again now demanded to know what was going on. Mary bit her lip nervously, looking away from him, "It's the train-," she couldn't believe she was about to really say this, "this train is… alive," she whispered, before adding hastily, "and speaking to me."

Mary could hardly bring herself to look at Alexander's face. She felt embarrassed. There's no way she would ever live this down. Against her better judgement, she quickly glanced up at Alexander's face and immediately regretted ever saying anything. She just about resisted the urge to face-palm herself, and briefly wished a black hole would appear out of nowhere to help her disappear. But then Mary wasn't sure she'd particularly enjoy being spaghettified to one atom thick or whatever Mr Spac, the physics teacher, had said.

She continued to stare adamantly out of the window, as Alexander, whose eyebrows were still scrunched up in worry, replied, "I really think you're getting barmy." He paused before continuing, "Maybe it's some sort of auditory hallucination. I mean, how can you have heard it speaking and I'm sitting right beside you, and I haven't heard anything? Besides, we live in the real world. Trains don't speak."

Great, thought Mary, *my bestie thinks I'm off my rockers,* she mentally rolled her eyes and kept herself deadly focused on staring outside at the blurred view she had seen hundreds of times before like it was the first time she'd ever seen outside. *Or the last*, a little voice in the back of her head thought, thinking up all the thrillers she'd seen, where people were locked away forever, to become the subjects of scary stories, after uttering crazy nonsense like, well- *'the talking train is alive'.* Mary grimaced at how absurd that sounded in her own mind. She suddenly felt very grateful that she was living in a century, where she wouldn't be immediately, and eternally, institutionalised after saying what she had just said.

The old lady, who had noticed that Mary's expression had changed and that she appeared to be speaking to herself again, shook her head and tutted, "The poor thing," under her breath. "Teenagers these days are really struggling with relationships, they've gone mad over each other." She sighed disapprovingly and returned, once again, to look out of the window.

Mary huffed, she couldn't have her best friend thinking she was crazy, not on her watch. Turning to him she said, "Alexander, let me prove I'm not crazy. If you don't believe me, no one else will." He looked at her with one eyebrow raised, with a mixture of concern and amusement. She ignored his questioning expression. She had an idea. Reaching out to the train, she made a request, "Please let my friend, Alexander, hear your voice too. Only then will he be able to believe that I'm not going crazy." Before she could stop herself, she added even more quietly than before, "and because I still think I'm going crazy myself…" she admitted, trailing off.

Determinate was only too happy to oblige. Besides, he could have a little *fun* with this. "Sure, I can," he said, tauntingly, "do you mean your *boyfriend*?"

Mary's breath faltered briefly, before she snapped, "Shut up! You stupid train! No, he's not!"

"Methinks the woman doth protest too much," Determinate replied teasingly. He had heard one of the other teens anxiously repeating this Shakespearean quote from the play Hamlet, over, and over again one morning. He must have had an English Literature assessment that day, it sounded incredibly stressful to Determinate.

Mary scowled, before smirking, "Okay, first of all, what century are you from? You're quoting Shakespeare, you must be *ancient*," she ridiculed. Still smirking, she went on, "and for your information, train, it's actually *'the lady doth protest too much, methinks'*. If you're going to quote Shakespeare at least quote him right," she grinned.

Suddenly, Determinate understood why the same teen might have been in such a foul mood about two weeks later when they had gotten their assessment results. *Oh dear.* Switching his attention back to the present, he goaded, "I know that you two fancy each other, but neither of you wants to be the first to say it. You are practically *lovebirds!*"

Mary blushed, failing to prevent herself from nervously smiling, she shook her head, as if to shake the thoughts away before almost angrily whispering, "Shut up, and get on with it!"

Determinate made a mental note to ask Mary if *"shut up"* was her favourite phrase, she seemed to use it excessively. Perhaps it was her first words as a baby, so she has a sentimental attachment to them. Determinate hypothesised; he was curious, and he would have to remember to ask.

"Yes, I do fancy him," Mary continued, "and so what? Don't tell him anything and mind your own business!" she said threateningly, in a very low voice so Alexander wouldn't hear. Determinate found it hilarious that this little human was attempting to threaten him. He was almost tempted to ask what exactly Mary had in mind to do, but he wasn't sure how much winding up Mary could take in one day.

Getting back to business, the train spoke to Alexander, "Hi, Alexander, Mary isn't going crazy. I'm alive, I speak and only those who I want to hear my voice can hear me."

Alexander's eyes became as wide as saucers. They both looked at each other in silence. Determinate noticed that their hearts were beating furiously. In fact, it oddly sounded as fast as those who had just nervously stolen their first kisses on the train. Determinate remembered how he had worried that someone was about to have a heart attack the first time he had heard such a reckless heartbeat. Determinate still wasn't a fan of public displays of affection after all these years, but he suspected that Alexander wouldn't mind as much.

Determinate went on to share with Alexander that he had also spoken to little Johnny and Alvin. However, he admitted that Alvin had run away when Determinate had tried to speak to him.

"I don't blame him!" Mary whispered, whilst Alexander chimed in nervously, "I feel like running away too."

"How is this even real?" Mary asked, thinking about how the train was too old to have any sort of voice control technology. In fact, Mary recalled that Alexander had recently done research about this sort of technology, and found that it was only invented a few years ago!

"I suppose this is a little strange," chuckled Determinate, sensing an odd moment of tension. "There are lots of mysteries about me."

Mary was still feeling uncertain that any of this was even happening for real. Perhaps she was just super stressed about this homework? Or she was dreaming? But after being seen speaking to herself, she had no intention of also being seen pinching herself to check her last idea. Once again, the train interrupted her thought process, saying, "I could help you with your maths homework if you would give me a moment of your time."

Mary's eyebrows raised and a small, excited smile crossed her face. "Can you?" she asked hopefully.

Alexander was intrigued by this, "I know all the formulas, let's see if you are also an intelligent train," this was a test for Determinate, but he was confident.

"I am indeed! I have already seen that Mary is a little confused with the formulas in her homework. From my stored data, I can tell you that the Pythagorean theorem states that in any right-angled triangle, the square length of the longer side, called the hypotenuse, is equal to the sum of the square lengths, of the other two sides that form the right angle."

As Alexander sat gawking in astonishment, Mary was also surprisedly staring at her homework sheet, as the questions on her page suddenly started to make a lot more sense. They even seemed solvable!

"I get it now," she gasped, "I wasn't squaring the other two sides!" She could hardly believe what she was experiencing. "Thanks," Mary said absent-mindedly as she had already begun furiously scratching down her work as if there was a time limit on how long the page would make sense.

"You are most welcome," replied Determinate, knowing Mary hadn't heard him at all.

Later, as Mary was getting off the train, Determinate asked, "Mary, just a second. Do you think you could organise for yourself, Alexander, Alvin and Johnny to meet up one day?"

"No one likes me," Mary scoffed in response, "I'm not the best person to do that. Ask Alexander or someone else to do it! Sorry," she said rushing away.

That weekend, Determinate had pondered on how he could manage to get the four of them together, so he could speak to them all at the same time. Not only did he have to figure out how to do that, but he also had to figure out a better way to get Alvin to understand what was happening. His best option looked like he might need the help of little Johnny. Luckily, he knew he would see them both on the Monday morning train.

When Monday morning came around, Johnny was super excited to catch the train. He took his seat in the front of the train, as always, and almost immediately began whispering in a low voice, "Train, can you hear me?"

"Yes, Johnny, I can hear and see you," Determinate responded humorously. "How are you today?"

"Fine, thank you," responded Johnny, gleefully.

Determinate could only imagine how many times the poor boy probably wondered if he had imagined this whole thing over the weekend.

"Johnny, can I ask you a very big favour today?" started Determinate. Johnny was already nodding. "Last week, I also tried to speak to moody Mary, Alexander and old Alvin. However, when I tried to speak to Alvin, he got a bit scared and ran away." He paused, to allow the young boy to process what he had just said. Then he continued, "When Alvin comes, ask him to sit across from you. Then ask him whether he remembers his name being called three times on Tuesday night when he was getting off the train. Let him know that it was me," Determinate instructed.

"I'll do it!" Johnny exclaimed enthusiastically, "but you have to promise me that you'll slow down when we pass the rainbow mountain this time. It's the most beautiful mountain I have ever seen. I'm always in a good mood when I look at it."

Determinate agreed to this, it was only fair. Determinate watched amused, as the little boy skilfully threw his thin, blue schoolbag onto the seat across from him. Johnny was certainly a quick thinker.

As the train approached the platform at the next station, Johnny quickly scanned the crowd to find old Alvin. He finally saw him slowly rising from a bench getting ready to board the train. As Alvin climbed aboard, Johnny called out to the older man,

"Over here, Mr Alvin!" As the older man turned around to face Johnny, Johnny excitedly pointed to the seat across from him. "I have put my school bag on this seat, to save it for you!" he beamed.

"Thank you very much, Johnny. You are a little angel, aren't you?" the old man chuckled, slowly walking towards the seat. "You are a very kind child!"

Johnny couldn't help the wide grin overtaking his face. Johnny's Mum looked over at Alvin, smiling and saying good morning, sitting a few seats behind Johnny, just as she did most mornings.

When Alvin was sitting comfortably and the train had continued chugging on, Johnny pounced into action. "Mr Alvin, did you hear someone calling your name on Tuesday night, by any chance?" he asked tentatively.

Alvin looked at Johnny aghast. "How do you know about *that,* boy? I didn't utter a single word to anyone. I've been ever so worried about it since it happened!"

he confessed. "I thought my little noggin' was finally giving up on me, I did!" he exclaimed, briefly distracted.

Johnny noticed how as the older man had raised his eyebrows, more wrinkles had appeared across his forehead. Johnny felt that the number of wrinkles must have doubled, but he resisted the urge to count. Nodding in reassurance, little Johnny leaned towards Alvin saying, "I'm going to tell you something, but you have to promise not to be afraid?"

"No," interrupted Alvin firmly, shaking his head at the young boy. Before Johnny could even attempt to continue, Alvin offered an unsolicited explanation for Tuesday night's shenanigans. "Wait, I bet it was the night guard trying to scare me off," he suggested, pointing an accusatory finger at a very empty seat as if he were currently reprimanding the accused mischief-maker sitting there.

Johnny shook his head, eager to clear the poor night guard's name. "No, Mr Alvin," he responded, "it was actually the train that called out to you. This train is alive! It really is," the boy explained, his excitement clearly seen by his large, exaggerated gesturing.

"Nonsense, boy," Alvin huffed, frowning. This boy had clearly been reading far too many fairy tales for his own good. "The train can't be alive, that's fairy tale business," Alvin insisted. What on earth were they teaching the children in school these days? He was much too old for such talk.

"Okay, let's prove it," suggested Johnny.

"How?" asked Alvin rather shortly, caught between feeling cross and wanting to humour the boy.

`"Let's ask the train to stop somewhere it has never stopped," proposed little Johnny slyly. Johnny already knew that he had this debate in the bag! Since Alvin seemed to have no objections, Johnny, with a small crafty smirk, made his proposition. "Train, if *you* called Alvin, can you stop at the open zoo so we can see the lions and tigers this morning?" Johnny was happy to see the older man nod in agreement with this suggestion. After all, no one had ever experienced the train stopping there.

Alvin was surprised that a small part of him wanted what the boy proposed to actually happen if only to prove that this was all true. Otherwise, he would have to seriously confront the sobering idea that he may really be losing his mind! As the train began slowing down as it passed by the rainbow mountain, Alvin's eyes began to open wider and wider. He found himself feeling a bundle of nerves with all the growing suspense. Alvin would never even dream that Johnny and the train had already agreed on this matter. As they began approaching the open zoo, Johnny and Alvin couldn't be more different. Whilst Johnny had progressed from fidgety with impatience, to practically bouncing in his seat in excited anticipation for the train to stop, Alvin was becoming increasingly terrified, as the train slowed to a halt right where the boy had asked.

The train finally came to rest at the open zoo, standing there for a minute before slowly chugging on again, so that all the other passengers would stop worrying and asking the train driver if the train had broken down. Determinate deduced from the train driver's frantic movements that the driver himself was shocked. It was understandable, Determinate thought because in the forty years the driver had been in this career, no train had ever stopped there. Everyone had been relieved when the train finally started with a jolt again. Everyone but Johnny, who was aware of exactly what was happening, and Alvin, who was lost in his own world. Although Alvin had been hoping for this outcome just moments ago, there was now a terrifying chance that reality was no longer real. And a disturbing chance that they were all aboard an alien train. At 60 years old, Alvin was finally having an existential crisis!

Alvin turned to stare at Johnny wide-eyed; he had started to believe this young boy, but he didn't want to. He had to ask a few more questions for confirmation. Alvin thought hard about what he wanted to ask before he came up with the perfect one. The train being able to speak at all was surprising, but it would be even more surprising if the train could answer this question, "If you are *really* real, what were my late parent's names?"

Without hesitation, Determinate responded, "Paige and Garfield were very nice people."

Alvin was chuffed. "You're right," he agreed, beaming with a sense of pride. Not only was this train smart, Alvin thought, but it also showed impressive skills in judging character.

Little Johnny's voice snapped him out of his distant thoughts. Johnny was informing Alvin that there was another secret. What more could there possibly be? Thought Alvin. This was already all so surreal!

"Only four of us can hear the train. No one else can!"

"That's amazing," replied Alvin initially. Then he questioned, "Hang on, who are the other two?"

"Moody Mary and her boyfriend, Alexander," the little boy giggled.

What a risky choice, thought Alvin to himself. The train had definitely gotten itself stuck in a giggle-worthy situation, choosing Mary. Because she wasn't exactly the most social character.

Once again, Alvin's thoughts were interrupted by what the train proposed as a *'small request'* of them both. Could they arrange a meeting together with Mary and Alexander, so that he could share something very, very important with the four of them? The train had stressed repeatedly, that they must be present to hear altogether, at the same time. Alvin found it almost comical that the train could classify anything to do with moody Mary as a '*small request.*' Regardless, little Johnny and Alvin both agreed on their plan to sit next to moody Mary that evening on the train home. Both were somewhat scared that this effort would prove fruitless and might just result in them getting told off by Mary.

The weekdays worked like clockwork. At around 3.45 pm little Johnny's Mum would have picked him up from school, walked to the train station, ready to board the train. Mary and Alexander would always be in hot pursuit, catching the train a mere 15 minutes later, when college was finished. Last but not least, just half an hour later, at around 4.30 pm, Alvin would also be on the train home from work. To keep things interesting, Determinate liked to think of this as a race, even though he already knew the outcome. That evening would be no exception, apart from Alvin and Johnny sitting next to Mary and Alexander, as planned and agreed.

Conveniently, they had all boarded the same front carriage together that evening. Little Johnny asked his Mum if he could sit beside Alvin again, and after checking with Alvin, who confirmed that he was okay with this, Johnny's Mum agreed. So, Johnny sat next to Alvin, with Mary and Alexander seated in front of them, separated by the table, occupied by Alexander's laptop, as usual.

It didn't take long for Mary to start getting very suspicious that they were all suddenly sitting so close. She sighed grimacing at the idea that they might be so *conveniently* placed, *to talk* to her. Immediately Mary's face twisted into a deep scowl. She really hated anything that encroached on her personal space. As the anxious knot began forming and growing in her tummy, Mary started to feel shyer. Unexpectedly, Johnny, the usually bounding, confident boy, was silently sharing Mary's sentiment. Alvin, eager to overcome the tension, stepped up to the challenge, asking Mary first, "How was school today? Both of you. All good?"

"Fine, thank you, Mr Alvin," replied Mary hesitantly.

Alexander, on the other hand, didn't even answer Alvin. He seemed to be away with the fairies. By this point, little Johnny had regained his usual courage and he could hardly wait to join the conversation. So much so, that before anyone else had the chance to speak, he happily began to tell Mary and Alexander about the train's request to have a meeting with them altogether. Mary internally rolled her eyes, at how quickly the stupid-smart train had managed to curate this meeting after she had declined the opportunity to help.

The train who had been listening too, and seeing everything, then interjected announcing his presence with greetings, "Hello Mary, Alexander, Alvin and Johnny," Determinate said, addressing them all individually. "Whilst I'm very happy that we have finally been able to meet, I'm afraid this isn't a social event, unfortunately. There is a very urgent situation at hand, so we have no time to waste. For 200 years, I have waited for this moment, eager to help humanity with all its intelligence problems. I have contacted you all because, from this point forward, I would like you guys to be the new A.I.I. team."

"What's that?" they all asked simultaneously.

"The 'Artificial Intelligence Investigators,'" Determinate clarified.

"But we don't know anything about investigating," complained Mary. They all nodded in agreement. Encouraged that she wasn't alone in her scepticism, Mary continued voicing her opinion more confidently, "We're just trying to wrap our minds around the whole concept of a talking train. That's more than enough by itself! Let alone prancing around pretending to be the tech FBI detective vigilantes, as you're suggesting!"

"I'm too old," agreed Alvin.

"Yeah, and I'm too young," chimed in little Johnny.

"What would our task be?" asked Alexander, earning incredulous looks from his team-mates. Alexander was on a totally different wavelength. He thought that this sounded too exciting to pass up. How many people would ever be able to say they had an opportunity to become a new type of secret agent, working for a talking train? They would be trend setters! With all the stars in his eyes, Alexander missed the look Alvin and Johnny shared before staring surprisedly at him. They couldn't begin to understand why Alexander was even *considering* this. Maybe because he was a computer wizard, who understood all about the world of Artificial Intelligence (AI) and its systems, he felt more confident with this idea, they wondered.

"Over the past couple of years, the police have had many unsolved mysteries concerning missing trains," Determinate started. "Those cases have all gone cold, because the police have no leads, but I might have some of the answers."

"I thought those trains just broke down and were out of action," Alvin muttered. "That's what all the public reports said, the police reports, local newspaper reports, and even on the information page on the train company's website."

"No, that's not true," Determinate replied. "I overheard the authorities talking about the missing train cases, and they are still trying to investigate but they are very confused. They don't know where the trains have gone, or who might have possibly taken them. Their main, and only real theory is that the construction industry might be stealing the trains and breaking them down, to profit from their steel and other metal parts. However, they haven't found any evidence of this so far."

"No one told us this," said Alvin.

Then, after a brief pause, Mary and Johnny asked, "What do *you* think happened to the trains?"

With a quick sigh, Determinate admitted that he had been keeping his eyes and ears keen on this situation ever since the first missing train, nine decades ago. In that case, Determinate still couldn't seem to find any answers. "But I do have answers to the local missing farm animals, the cows, bulls, sheep, pigs and horses that have gone missing," he commented.

That news definitely piqued the team's interest and the train now had everyone's undivided attention.

"All our families have missing animals!" said Alexander, whilst the other two nodded. They appeared to Determinate oddly similar to a pair of inanimate bobble-head figurines on a dashboard, rather than nodding humans.

Alvin sighed recalling out loud how everyone, including the local police, thought this was all the work of a thief probably from the neighbouring village. Or the other theory circulating in the local gossip, that it could be a pack of stray dogs who they hadn't caught yet.

"What a plausible theory!" Mary guffawed, her words dripping with sarcasm. "Stray dogs, taking down bulls and horses, more than twice their size and leaving no trace." She rolled her eyes throwing herself back in her seat with a huff. Alexander thought he heard an almost inaudible, "bunch of idiots…" leave Mary's lips under her breath. It was so quiet he wasn't even sure he had really heard anything.

The train would have shaken his head if he had one. "No, it definitely wasn't a person, or a pack of dogs," Determinate confirmed. Whether he wanted to admit it or not, he was actually with moody Mary on this one. He too, couldn't even begin to fathom *how* dogs could possibly steal farm animals, not to mention trains, entirely unnoticed. It was preposterous, but Determinate decided against questioning their logic with this at this particular time.

"Listen carefully," Determinate resumed, in an attempt to bring everyone's mind back from going off on that tangent. "The animals were taken by-" he paused struggling to find the most fitting words to describe the sight. "-it was a *creature* but with some machine-like features too," Determinate described, but it sounded more like it was almost a question. Deciding to just go with it, he continued, "It was one of a kind. Well, at least, I've never seen anything like it before! It almost felt like it was from another world," he paused again, this time to allow the team to truly absorb this new information.

After a few minutes, Determinate continued, "It made its first appearance fifty years ago. It only ever moves in the dead of night, taking the animals, when everyone else is asleep." The group sat silently. No one even looked at each other. They were all so caught up in their fear and alarm, trying to digest this news.

Johnny nervously tried to crack a joke, "So… what you're saying is, at night, when not a creature is stirring, not even a mouse… a transformer appears and starts stealing animals and trains…"

Mary, who was at this point in a bit of a foul mood, glared at Johnny silencing him back into his restless mind. "Now isn't the time to experiment with Dr Seus, Johnny," she snapped.

"Sorry," said Johnny embarrassed. It wasn't long before he too was lost in his own thoughts, staring absentmindedly at a small scrap of paper that had clearly seen better days on the train floor.

"What if it starts coming for us when it's finished taking all of the animals?" Mary gasped. If Determinate was right, the world as they knew it was caving in; there was a massive, very real threat looming over them.

"That's what we will be trying to stop as the A.I.I. team," Determinate encouraged. "This is a very important job. The four of you have a lot to consider. Don't be afraid, I'll be here helping you all the way. As the next stop is yours, why don't you all sleep on it, and we can continue this discussion tomorrow?"

They all agreed. Getting off the train all four of them felt tired, very afraid and worried. They tried their utmost to appear calm so no one would notice their fear, as they went their separate ways.

The next morning, the team were very anxious to catch the train to continue their discussions about the mysterious livestock-stealing creature, that could potentially also pose a threat to them! None of them could help their curiosity. It was like a car crash, you want to look away, but you just can't. They wanted to know the full description of the creature, to discover what exactly they might be up against, as well as more information on what exactly the train thought they were supposed to be doing next.

That whole night, even though they were all in the comfort of their own separate houses, they were united by the fact they were all wide awake, unable to find restful sleep. To any outsider looking in, it would appear that these individuals were simply star-gazing, but they were each discreetly on the look out to catch a glimpse of the creature.

When Determinate pulled into the station the next morning, it was very clear that none of his new friends had gotten nearly enough sleep last night; if their twitchiness and the bags under their eyes were anything to go by. Determinate felt a pang of guilt, maybe he had scared them too much? Or perhaps, after shattering their perception of reality, they had millions of unanswered questions that had probably kept them awake all night.

The four of them sat very close together. They were mindful to stay near little Johnny's mother, as Johnny wasn't allowed to sit out of her line of sight. The train waited until they were all seated comfortably, before continuing the previous day's conversation. To the other passengers, it looked as if the four were talking amongst themselves. They remained none-the-wiser about the strange communication taking place right before their very eyes.

Impatiently, Johnny launched his attack asking, "What does the creature look like? Your description was a little unclear yesterday." Mary, Alexander and Alvin sat quietly, eagerly awaiting the response too.

"Before I answer those questions," Determinate said pointedly, "beware that being involved with this team could be dangerous. It is a very big responsibility for you all; make sure that you stay vigilant and careful at all times." Determinate noticed how Alvin shuffled nervously in his seat, glancing down at little Johnny quickly, with a look of concern etched across his face. "But please try not to worry," the train reassured, "I'll give you all the knowledge you need to stop this creature before it begins to start taking humans."

Determinate went on to describe how difficult it was to put the creature's appearance into words. "It doesn't seem to have a set form, easily transforming and shifting from one appearance to another every time I have seen it. The first time I saw it, it was incredibly large, practically the size of an elephant, with an odd mix of features from both a wolf and a lion. It also had a large pair of wings, with sharp inescapable claws attached to the edge of them. Nothing could escape the grip of those things." The train rocked from side to side subtly as Determinate shivered, recalling the horrific sight.

"The second time that I saw it," Determinate continued "It walked upright on two legs, like a human. Like the first time, it had wings, except this time they projected from its body almost like a second pair of hands, again, with claws optimally positioned, ready to attack." Determinate paused, contemplating whether he wanted to divulge his next suspicion, but he saw little point in holding back now that the scariest parts, the reality, had already been discussed. "Perhaps, slightly more alarming is the fact that I have a growing suspicion that this creature potentially never leaves. What if this creature simply assumes the appearance of a normal human, and is just living among us during the day?" he finished. It was a good thing that was all the train had to say, because everyone's face became ashen, and every pair of eyes held a similar distant expression.

Before they arrived at their destinations, Determinate discussed his main strategy with them. He had relayed how he had noticed that the creature seemed to always have wings regardless of appearance. He proposed that they should start their investigation by focusing on anyone that always seems to be carrying extra loads on their back – potentially hiding their wings. Determinate had suggested that this could look like someone wearing large coats, or someone always carrying very big bags on their backs. In addition, he had proposed that it might be a good idea to also keep an eye out for a person who didn't seem to eat, a person that always seemed to be missing at night, and most importantly, any person that seemed to be completely unconnected to the community. For example, someone who didn't have any family history or doctor's records.

"The quest to save our village and the nearby towns is now in your hands. Try to get the local police inspectors on your team," Determinate advised them before they left.

Determinate knew from their contemplative silences and dejected expressions that they didn't feel like they were cut out for this task. However, after analysing them, he thought their combined skills made them an ideal team. He saw great potential in them. Despite Alvin being in his 60s, he was still very strong, intelligent, and trustworthy. He was incredibly responsible, never straying far from his moral compass, choosing to do what was right, even when it wasn't always necessarily the easiest option.

Meanwhile, despite all of Mary's shyness, social anxieties and short temper, and under all those thick layers of sarcasm, she always took care to be helpful and mindful of others. Most people didn't notice how she often stopped to help the elderly on and off the trains. But Determinate most certainly did. She had a brilliantly creative, punctual, and dedicated character. Alexander complemented Mary perfectly with his more peaceful aura, as well as his equally brilliant inclination towards a more faithful, thoughtful, punctual and meticulous disposition. Mary could always trust Alexander to be there for her, especially with any technology troubles! He was incredibly talented in all things to do with ICT. If there was anyone who could research, develop, implement and fundamentally resolve an issue with an Artificial Intelligence (AI) system, it would be him.

In addition, the team was equipped with yet another genius. Although very few people knew this, at just 9 years old, little Johnny had demonstrated an IQ equivalent to that of a university student. Johnny was also a kind, courageous, intelligent and inquisitive character with a knack for research. That came in very handy when Johnny needed to get to the bottom of something, such as a mystery. Like Mary, he also loved to help people. Although they weren't confident in themselves, Determinate could think of no one more suited to this great task than the four of them.

Together they had to work out and plan some sort of regular meeting, scheduled at a set location, that would allow them to share and discuss any new updates or information together as a group. The team pondered for a while, struggling to come up with any feasible options before Alvin had a bright idea,

"I was a teacher for 20 years," he explained, "so, I can open a 'tutoring' class to 'tutor' all of you as my students. That gives us the perfect excuse to all meet up at the same time and place for few hours each week. What do you think of that?" he asked, hopefully.

"That's a good idea," agreed Mary, followed by Alexander and Johnny. "But how will we get the train close enough for us to communicate?" she asked, slightly faltering on the word communicate. She still hadn't quite figured out how to classify whatever was happening between them and the train.

"We should try to rent one of the empty offices at one of the train yards," suggested Alvin. "You know, where some of the trains rest in the evenings."

Everyone agreed that this was a great idea. So, Alvin went to acquire the office space for his evening and weekend 'tutoring' classes. Inspired by Determinate's suggestions, he named his new company the 'A.I.I. Tutoring School.' Alvin chuckled realising everyone would assume the name was made up of his initials, instead of representing 'Artificial Intelligence Investigator,' as it did.

Alvin had managed to find the perfect office space, on the ground floor, where Determinate and the team would be able to hear and communicate with one another. He had actually been lucky enough to secure the office at a significantly discounted rate because it was so close to the train track that no one would usually consider it because of all the potential noise pollution. With their plans made a reality, everyone agreed to meet for 'tutoring' as previously discussed.

Together they had also managed to formulate a step-by-step plan to commence their investigation. They were confident that they had a winning plan to get the police inspector on their team, but the million-dollar-question on all their minds was, *'could they be confident in the police team?'* More specifically, could the inspector be trusted with Determinate's secret? What if the police inspector *was* the creature? How could they be sure?

Determinate was happy with all the plans the team had agreed upon; now it was time to begin actioning them. They would start by undertaking careful surveillance of all the villagers. They would be keeping an eye out for anyone appearing to potentially be trying to hide wings under their coat or bags.

"See you all tomorrow," Determinate said one evening, excusing himself back to the train yard for the night and leaving the team to continue working on their own for a while as they usually did. Every week he was pleased with their focus and dedication to this project. Whether they had a good week of leads and clues or not, they remained determined with a positive outlook.

Before Determinate could even begin chugging off, Alexander quickly called out to the train, hurriedly sweeping all his papers off of the desk and into his rucksack. "Wait, I'll come with you! Can you please drop me off at my stop? I'll catch up with the team tomorrow, but I need to go home, my mum is waiting for me."

Alexander missed the flash of sadness that briefly danced across Mary's face. She loved his company and hated how she could hardly concentrate when he was gone. Even after Alexander was gone, Mary stared wistfully into space, wishing she would finally have the courage to tell him that she liked him… a lot. Next time I see him I'll just go for it, she reasoned with herself. Whether the feeling was mutual or not *"Que sera, sera"* what will be, will be, this was up to her.

While they were travelling back home, the troublesome train teased Alexander, "I can see that you really like Mary, so… when are you going to tell her?" If he had had eyebrows, Determinate would have used this opportunity to attempt mimicking wiggling them, the way he had seen passengers do so effortlessly several times before. "You shouldn't wait too long with these sorts of things, you know," he urged.

Alexander looked away hesitantly. He paused. Taking a breath he said somewhat bravely, "I was actually planning on telling her tomorrow, with a surprise gift. That's why I want to get home quickly. I asked my mum to buy it for me today whilst she was out shopping. Now I'm going home to look at it."

The nervous tinge had barely left his cheeks when Determinate jeered again "That's fantastic, magpie-sorry I meant, *Alexander,* you are a *very* thoughtful young man."

He didn't need a mirror to know that his face was rapidly becoming shy again. 'Magpie', the village's ship-name for the couple, usually had that effect on him when Alexander was confronted with it. He didn't bother responding to the cheeky train, he wasn't sure just how many cheeky comments it might have accumulated over the years! Alexander would let it slide, for now, but he would get the train back, eventually…

As Determinate was approaching the railway switch, an obscure, intense, bright light appeared in the midst of the railway switch. Determinate sincerely hoped that Alexander's eyes were firmly closed, it was far too bright for human eyes. Briefly, he became aware of Alexander's presence crouching behind a seat to shield himself from the violent light. Reassured that Alexander was trying to brace himself for any potential impact, Determinate tried to redirect his attention to applying the brakes as hard as he could, in an attempt to stop them from merging into this explosive light.

Neither Determinate, nor Alexander, blinded by the light, could see that not only was the light surreally bright, but it was growing. Around the bend, between two small mountains, no one else would witness the light continuing to expand at an alarming speed. The tufts of greenery scattered about the mountain swayed, moved about by the force emitted from the light. As it continued to expand, small stones and loose soil were displaced, and blown away by the force; small animals and birds fled to safety. It seemed there would be no stopping, as it continued to surge violently on roots, twigs and stones that clambered together performing their percussion symphony. It was chaos, and then abrupt stillness, as everything was plunged back into a familiar darkness. The shrubbery and loose stones lay wherever they had fallen, littered around the mountain area haphazardly. Everything was accounted for, everything but Determinate with Alexander. If mountains could speak, they would relay an unimaginable story of a train being swallowed up into a bright light, as if the train was simply a speck of sand.

The next morning, Alvin walked up to the platform ready to clue everyone in on the final details they had discussed after the train had returned the day before. He was distracted from his thoughts by some commotion towards the entrance of the station. Hobbling a little closer to the station's entrance for a clearer view, Alvin could make out the figures of the train inspectors and the police at the station having a meeting in the distance. *I wonder what's happening?* He thought. He could see that Mary and Johnny were already over there, along with lots of other worried people.

Alvin wandered over to them. "What's the matter?" he asked.

"I'm not sure," Mary replied, "but the train seems to be running late this morning."

Alvin saw the worried expression that Mary tried to hide from him. Instinctively, he glanced at his watch. Mary was right, the train was running late. That train was never late, he thought, meeting eyes with Mary briefly. Alvin shook his head as if to shake the anxiety out of them both. He nodded his head toward the inspectors, encouraging Mary and Johnny to accompany him to speak to them. "Let's find out for sure, shall we?"

"Good morning, Inspector, we were just wondering what time the train will be coming this morning?" asked Alvin.

"Morning," replied the inspector curtly. "We're dealing with multiple issues this morning, but we can assure you that we'll have you on your way soon, Sir. There will be a bit of a delay," the inspector said in an almost robotic voice. Alvin could only assume that the poor man had faced the same question one too many times today already! He looked so fed up that Alvin almost regretted having questioned him at all!

"What caused all this?" he nevertheless continued to ask. "Do you know?"

The vein in the inspector's forehead stood out as he shot a warning glance at Alvin. Little Johnny subconsciously leaned away from him. That man was certainly in a foul mood. Alvin looked away under the intensity of the laser beams being fired at him. Hopefully, his question would be answered more informatively this time, because he wasn't entirely sure the Inspector wouldn't attempt to arrest him on the charge of irritation at this present moment.

With a huff, the Inspector muttered, "The delay has been caused by the old train – the one that's late now - breaking down on the way here this morning. Whilst we are making every attempt to get you all back on your journeys as swiftly as possible, I'm sure you'll understand that with a current missing person's investigation, this isn't our sole or top priority. However, we are working hard to clear the train lines to get you back on journeys as soon as possible," he reassured dismissively, with a patronising half-smile and running a hand over his beard before walking away.

"But that's my absolute favourite train!" cried Johnny, in the direction of the Inspector's retreating back. He and Mary shared a worried look. Mary patted Johnny's shoulder in an effort to soothe him, whilst her own lips were pulled taut into a thin line with the very same growing panic.

The Inspector faltered in step slightly, but without turning around he responded in a softer tone, "Everyone loved that old train," he nodded, "but the old thing probably needs some new parts, which we're unsure of whether we can get our hands on, or how long it would take for this particular train. I wouldn't hold my breath if I were you, I'm afraid," he said, miraculously reanimating his attitude-infused tone. Alvin only vaguely registered the change; he had quickly forgotten the Inspector's rotten attitude. His mind was spinning with questions.

Mary's head tilted to the left slightly as another worrisome wave washed over her; she didn't like anything coming out of the Inspector's mouth, and it had nothing to do with his tone. Firstly, they were suggesting that the train had broken down, but there were so many officers there, it wasn't adding up. Not to mention it was the same false explanation they had given for the other trains that hadn't broken down but were literally missing; and the fact that he had said 'loved,' past tense. Mary sighed in frustration, running her fingers through her hair. *Did the creature take the train? If so, what were they supposed to do without him?* She was NOT ready for this!

At the same time, Alexander's parents were caught in an awkward half-run half-walk motion hurrying into the station. The thinly-veiled panic could be seen in their robotic strained movements. Like a mirror, the team found themselves becoming just as tense. As tight knots began forming in their stomachs, they all waited silently to hear what the parents had to say. The cloudy skies overhead had never looked so foreboding, something was definitely wrong. The Salvadors beelined to Mary as she stood by Alvin and little Johnny. Immediately, the parents launched a barrage of questions at Mary. "*Where is he? Did he stay overnight at your house? When was the last time you saw him? What time exactly was that?*" The Salvadors' growing panic was infectious. Mary, shook her head "No! Who? Alexander!?" The parents continued staring at her without a word. "-he went home early yesterday evening, he caught the evening train about 5 pm," she said all in one breath.

A pained expression spread across Mrs Salvador's face as she clutched at her chest. "My son's missing, my son's missing," she muttered in shock and worry. Mary's face drained of colour; Alexander was *missing.* Her magpie was missing. Sounds began to blend together fading in the distance as a worried tear rolled down Mrs Salvador's face in slow motion. It only took a few minutes for the other villagers to bring Mary back to consciousness. It took a lot longer for Mary to stop feeling as if she was free-falling into a pit of despair.

When the information sunk in, Mary collected herself and cautiously asked, "Didn't he come home last night at all? Did he call? Did you call him? What did he say?"

"He left his phone at home in the morning and we thought he was with you," replied Mr Salvador, "so we were not worried. We went to sleep. But we realised in the morning that he hadn't slept in his bed and did not come home at all. Therefore, we made our way to the station to check on you both and make sure he went to College." Mr Salvador's voice faded as he was going through the information once again and realising how unrealistic it sounded. A look of despair crossed his face and that of Mrs Salvador and Mary.

Similar expressions danced across all of the other's faces as if they were sharing exactly the same thought. But who could blame them? Additionally, to Mary, Johnny and Alvin, it was awfully suspicious that just after breaking its silence, to give them a heads up about a train-snatching, animal-stealing creature lurking about, 'their' train was suddenly "broken down." After two *hundred* years, the train had *"conveniently"* broken down, after providing them with valuable information to help them defend themselves in this real-life version of the 'Among Us' game they were in; what a *coincidence*!

Even more troubling, one of their own, Alexander, had now suddenly gone missing. Mary stared miserably into the distance. She willed Alexander to just appear on the horizon, run up to them huffing and puffing with some idiotic story to explain this vanishing act. It was better than the horrible thought crossing her mind, of Alexander, clutched in the claws of some giant mutant animal thing. She shuddered at those mental images. He'd better have fallen in a ditch with a broken ankle somewhere with no signal or WiFi and a new pet rabbit or something, she thought angrily. Alexander wouldn't want her to get lost in thinking the worst, so she wouldn't.

Alvin felt it was time to assume the role of the authority figure, and take control right now. He for one was unconvinced by the whole "broken down" scenario. He spoke up first, "We have to investigate this," he encouraged. "I have been getting this train since I was a young boy going to school, and it's never stopped or broken down!"

Mary and Johnny nodded in agreement. Alvin was glad that they at least had each other to talk to about this because they wouldn't be able to share any of this with anyone else. It was crucial for them to be in unison, especially if Alvin's hunch was true. He suspected that there was a strong possibility that whoever, or *whatever*, took the train, also took Alexander, when they left yesterday.

"We can do this," Mary agreed, encouraging the rest of the team as well as herself. "I'll do everything in my power to find my Alexander. Besides, he is well aware that I haven't given him permission to escape me just yet. He'll have to try much harder to lose me!"

Johnny stifled a giggle, side-eyeing the teen. If he wasn't sure that Mary was in shock before, with the whole fainting scene, he was sure now. He concluded that as many of the books he had read had suggested, love really did make people a bit loopy.

The replacement train came shortly after and they all got on it. That morning's commute, although following the same route, felt alien to the new trio. An uncomfortably loud silence surrounded them for the whole duration of the journey. Alvin felt out of place. He hadn't imagined how isolating this would be. All the other villagers outside of the A.I.I team were so relaxed, blissfully ignorant of the mystery unfolding around them. Sure, he had heard one or two concerned whispers about Alexander's disappearance, but no one knew it was bigger than that, *much bigger*. The community didn't know there was anything to be concerned about, despite everything happening in front of their very eyes! It gave Alvin a sickly mix of disturbing and overwhelming him in the pit of his stomach, with the bitter taste of worry in his mouth. He felt forced to ponder how many times humans walked around oblivious to life-threatening danger clouding around them; it was another chilling and sobering thought. He had had one too many of those lately. He shook his head clearing his thoughts. It was up to the three of them to uncover the truth about what was happening and find Alexander. They had to do this on their own, but they would be successful, Alvin was so sure of this, he would bet his pension on it!

That afternoon, they all met up as usual at the 'A.I.I. Tutoring School' to discuss matters further. Everyone had wasted yet another day hopelessly distracted by thoughts and worries about what was happening. Mary couldn't count how many times she had been told off or teased for her obvious distraction today. Even the teachers were making '*magpie this*' and '*magpie that*' sorts of comments. By the end of lunch, there was a permanent death glare on her face for anyone who dared to even look her way for too long. Mary was glad no one could read her mind as there were a lot of Kung-Fu Panda-inspired scenes going on in her mind for all of those people. How else could she manage her stress and irritation? Besides, it kept her mind free from more disturbing fears for Alexander's safety.

Together, the team decided that the most logical first step would be to actually develop a plan to confirm their hypothesis that the train was missing instead of broken. If they found evidence to prove them right, it would also indicate a potential explanation for Alexander's disappearance. Everyone knew that a broken train could only be in one of two locations here, either at the old train yard or in the train engineer building waiting to be fixed. They all felt tempted to march straight over there and check the locations immediately. However, as Johnny reminded them, they had to resist that urge. They needed to be discreet. In order to investigate without arousing suspicion, they decided that they would have to wait two weeks. This would allow them to get permission to tour both locations under the guise of an "educational tour."

The fortnight had been a torturous wait for them, the longest of their entire lives. Thankfully, everything had been approved and they were able to freely tour both locations for their "educational trip." When they visited, it was just as they suspected. All the past and current trains were accounted for, but the old train was nowhere to be seen. They had put little Johnny in charge of taking photos. He was tasked with capturing as much evidence as possible, so they could be printed, viewed, and really scrutinised later, back at the tutoring school.

Later that week, they were back in the A.I.I. room, gathered around two desks, staring at the photos. Mary had never thought about working as an investigator, or anywhere in the law enforcement sector before. However, the tedious task of searching for clues when she had no idea what she was looking for, made her sure this field was not her cup of tea at all. As her eyes skipped from one image to another, the photos became a sum of random colour splurges in her field of vision. She began rubbing her eyes and temples and scratching her head. She took a five- minute comfort break and made herself some chamomile tea. She was frustrated as this felt pointless. Alexander had been missing for more than two weeks and they were nowhere closer to finding him. "This is for Alexander. This is for Alexander," she chanted, in her mind, over and over to motivate herself to get back to the task.

Moments later, Mary noticed something interesting in one of the photos. Through a window into one of the offices, they could just about see a notice board on the wall. There was part of a message clearly seen on it, but it was a bit like a decoding task to try to make it out because although you could see parts of the sentences, a lot of the message was obscured by the window frames. Who knew, solving word problems such as anagrams would feature as part of their investigation? But this was just what Mary needed, a bit of excitement in the form of a challenge; she had always been very good at word problems. Whilst Mary didn't know if any of the information on the board would help the investigation, she was committed to being the first one to solve this puzzle.

Hours flew by in what felt like seconds when Alvin finally interrupted the investigation, "It's getting dark now," he pointed out, "we should stop for today, and continue again tomorrow. Luckily, it's the weekend so we'll have more time to dedicate to solving this."

Stretching as they got out of their seats, Johnny and Mary noticed how weary they felt and how stiff their joints were. They couldn't agree more that it was probably time to throw in the towel and head home to rest up for tomorrow.

Saturday morning bright and early they were back at it, with freshly rested minds. Mary had solved most of the word puzzle the day before, and since there didn't seem to be many other leads, the trio put their skills together to crack the puzzle. The collective information understanding said:

"Attention ALL staff:

The following information must be kept covert.

We have another open missing train case, and a missing person case, namely, Alexander, 17 years old, male. Both appear to have gone missing around the same time. It is suspected that the missing person may have been onboard at the time of the train abduction.

The police are currently trying to investigate, however, there have been no leads. Please keep this information from the public. Thank you."

Johnny took a deep breath in as a chill went down his spine; it was starting to feel more real and serious by the second, and he didn't like the way it was headed at all. Whilst it was in a way good that they had evidence confirming what they were suspecting, Alvin found himself once again feeling unsettled about everything the village might be hiding from the people. A soft pattering noise caught his attention; he turned to look and was just in time to see the glimmer of sunlight catching the droplet of water collecting under Mary's chin, as she turned, her face away, crying. As he turned to look at Johnny, he too looked distressed, his small face hiding none of it.

"How are we going to find a trustworthy authority figure to actually help us with this situation? This is getting too dangerous to do alone," sniffled Mary.

"I don't know," Johnny replied solemnly before Alvin could speak, "but we have to find the train and Alexander."

Alvin had yet to respond. He paused, deeply considering something, "It might be a long shot, but I might know a former soldier. He was a great soldier, but he's on early retirement from service. I can trust him. He might be the only person we can call; actually, he might very well be the best serviceman to call."

Johnny nodded in acknowledgement, as an uncomfortable silence started overtaking the room.

After a couple of minutes, Mary, who had been staring teary-eyed out of the window, suddenly sat up a little straighter, swivelling around so hastily in her seat, Johnny considered it an act of violence against her spine. He winced disgustedly feeling a bit nauseous at the thought.

"I think I saw someone this morning with a big coat going into the town manager's office. It looked like he was wearing a rucksack underneath the coat. I'm not a hundred per cent sure," she stuttered, her words almost merging together in her haste to get them out, "but I guess it's worth investigating?"

It took a solid couple of minutes for Johnny and Alvin to figure out exactly what Mary had communicated in that mumble of sounds, but eventually, they did.

"It's definitely worth investigating," agreed Johnny. "It's our only lead."

Alvin nodded, "I can take a few days off work to investigate it. You kids focus on finishing your school term. There are only a few days left until the start of your summer holidays. We can definitely pick this up together and get more work done during the summer holidays to get to the bottom of this." He saw Mary was about to speak in protest, but before she could even get a word out, he continued, "That's non-negotiable, go home."

Like a lightning strike cutting against a dark colourful sky, Determinate felt the flash of light intensify, suddenly feeling ten times brighter and somehow faster. Then Determinate felt his wheels propelled forward slightly with the force of the flash towards the back of the train, before feeling like he was suddenly stationary on a train track again as if nothing had happened. For a second, Determinate felt relieved that whatever was happening had stopped, but what exactly had happened? Briefly, he entertained the idea that he had experienced a hallucination, similar to what humans experienced due to the lack of water in a desert. That idea faded as quickly as it came. For one, he wasn't convinced that trains could hallucinate, also what exactly was he lacking? His engine was full and the machinery was all working just fine so what train equivalent of human dehydration could he possibly have? Moreover, the presence of a racing heartbeat in his carriage solidified Determinate's doubt of that theory. There was just no way that a human, and a train, shared the same hallucination experience at the same time.

Focusing back on the heartbeat, Determinate called out to Alexander, "Are you ok? You didn't get hurt, did you?"

"No, I'm fine," the boy confirmed. "What happened? Where are we?" He sounded as confused as Determinate felt.

"I don't know," admitted Determinate distractedly. They were both trying to take in their surroundings to get their bearings after such a disorientating experience. With every passing second it was becoming very apparent, that they were no longer anywhere near the railway switch that they had been at, just seconds before. In fact, the more they looked around, the more it seemed that they were somewhere entirely new. Nothing looked familiar to either party; the skyline was littered with silhouettes of different shapes, colours and sizes of buildings. Obnoxious lights interrupted the natural evening sky. It didn't take an expert to identify that they were in a city, however, Alexander felt that he could greatly benefit from an expert explaining exactly how they had got there, right about now.

As they looked around the station more, their eyes were drawn to the many subtle details that they had previously overlooked in the quick scan of their surroundings. Firstly, the tops of the trees visible above the platform's walls looked like a surrealist's representation of a tree, it was so bizarrely disconnected from anything they had ever seen before. Staring at the trees, Determinate couldn't bring himself to think of them as real, they had to be fake right? Tree-themed art to add a bit of character to the city, but what city even did that? Or had the budget for it?

Also, on a lighting display board close by, was the strangest thing. It seemed to advertise what was supposedly a form of transport, but Determinate had never seen anything like it. As if that wasn't confusing enough, the text in the corner of the display induced more confusion. Although Determinate knew that he physically didn't have a heart, he would have sworn it had stopped temporarily seeing the date on the sign; it read '9022.' The rest of the text was indecipherable, being in an unknown language. Determinate tried to calm himself down, maybe he was in overdrive and seeing things?

"Can you see that sign in the lighting display Alexander?"

Without missing a beat, Alexander nodded. "I can also see it's dated 9022," Determinate could almost hear the restrained panic, trying to break through into his voice. "And the fact that's all I can read... What language is that anyway? I've never come across it."

"I was hoping you wouldn't say that, I have no idea what language that is," admitted Determinate.

Hearing that Alexander let out a big breath and then the panic bubbled over, "Where are we?!"

"We must be in the big city over the north side of the village. Maybe they're advertising an extravagant event or something which requires such an absurd advertising technique..." Determinate suggested, pausing for a second before adding, "or perhaps there was a malfunction in printing, but they decided to use the display anyway?"

Immediately Alexander trembled in frustration. "No, it's not. I visited the big city just last week with my parents. This isn't it at all," he said adding extra emphasis on the '*at all*'.

Suddenly, they were rudely interrupted from their worrisome thoughts, as Determinate felt himself being picked up and lifted clean off of the track. It was so unexpected, Alexander who had been standing mid-aisle, was immediately thrown to the floor, muttering an obscenity. Determinate could tell the moment Alexander realised what was happening, the boy's silence, his nails digging into the sides of the seat, and finally, Alexander sitting completely straight-spined, practically moulding himself into the seat. Alexander's reaction to heights was frightening. Determinate couldn't see what was picking him up, but he quickly came up with a plan to try to find out. He began to rock from side to side subtly so that Alexander wouldn't be flung around like a squash ball in the carriage, as well as to make it seem like a natural sway in the wind, rather than a conscious train trying to catch a glimpse of whatever was lifting him. The last thing they needed right now was for Determinate to be discovered as an AI train. It took a few sways to finally catch the glimpse he was working for, but he immediately wished he hadn't. What he saw could only be described as a monster, it seemed ten times bigger than him. They were being carried in the claws of a machine. This was NOT looking good.

"Alexander," Determinate whispered, "Alexander, don't say a word, a machine is carrying us, you need to hide in the toolbox compartment under the front seat, and don't come out until I call you. I'm going to shut my system down as well until I figure out what is going on. Go now," he instructed. Once Alexander had safely scrambled into the compartment and settled down, Determinate quickly shut his receiver and transmitter down; this way he could more effectively keep his AI system a secret. He discreetly kept watch as he continued to be hoisted higher and higher into the sky.

From this height, Determinate could see a perfectly uninterrupted view of the sea, rivers and sky. Unfortunately, instead of a spectacularly beautiful view, Determinate had to add this view to the list of things he wished he hadn't seen. Like a particularly disconcerting nightmare, the skyline was littered with several randomly positioned and coloured distant spheres.

Determinate nearly blew a fuse, just how high up did they have to go to be casually seeing planets? Reluctantly, he risked a glance towards the ground below, expecting some sort of strange aerial view of a continent, but they weren't halfway between the clouds and the rest of space like he imagined. Determinate wasn't sure what to make of the facts as they were appearing. How did any of this make any sense? Factoring all these components into the equation - the bright light, the spontaneous location change, the unrecognisable language, brash new buildings, the fact that there were luridly coloured planets casually visible across the sky, the odd appearance of the mountains, sea and rivers, as well as the strange different transport technology and the giant flying machine carrying them - it all pointed to one main theory, the bright light was a vortex, which sent them straight to an alternate world, or universe.

Determinate decided that he had had enough of seeing anything for now, how many unpleasant surprises would anyone like to experience all at once anyway? He wouldn't look at anything else until it was necessary.

When Determinate felt himself being lowered and finally put down again, he mustered up the courage to look at his surroundings. He saw what looked like a hybrid military base, with giant intimidating machines that Determinate honestly thought looked fatal to human life. He couldn't even fathom what any person would need such machinery for or what it could even be used for. It was almost like this military base wasn't meant for just humans, but for humans *and machines* to use. Listening closely, he heard multiple different conversations overlapping; slightly straining to focus his hearing, he discovered that these conversations seemed to be happening in many different languages. Surprisingly, Determinate could understand some of them, but there was also an unmistakable strange and unrecognisable-sounding foreign language being spoken. Perhaps that was what the strange language on the light display sounded like, possibly?

Something else had been bothering Determinate about this scene though, it took him a minute to figure out what was niggling at him. He realised that in fact there were distinctly more voices being heard than people around in the area. Focusing more intently, once again, because that would make no sense. Yet again, Determinate became astonished, it felt like this would be a common occurrence in this environment! There were more voices than people because it wasn't just *people* talking, all the machines and vehicles, including trains here, were openly communicating too! Determinate was dumbstruck. Sure, these vehicles were much newer, more advanced, and seemed far more intelligent than him, but Determinate felt a jolt of excitement there were finally more trains like him and he wasn't alone in the world. Or perhaps, it would be more accurate to say, he wasn't alone in this world specifically. Still looking around in amazement, Determinate's line of vision finally rested on the other missing trains from years ago, but they too were different; they had been upgraded and completely transformed! To say that Determinate was shocked and impressed would be an understatement.

The familiar sound of wheels rolling along the track stole his attention. He watched silently as a train came into view, speeding up more and more until it was hurtling down the track. Determinate wasn't keen on witnessing an accident today, but he just couldn't tear his eyes away from the pending catastrophe happening right in front of him. As the train gathered more and more momentum, the sound grew like a crescendo. The thundering echoes bounced off the walls; Determinate could hardly hear his own panicked thoughts over the ruckus, but he didn't mind much as he still couldn't make himself look away. Just when Determinate felt the volume had begun erring on the side of unbearable, there was a sudden silence. If Determinate had a jaw it would have become best friends with the floor at that very moment, because before his very eyes, the train had transformed into an aeroplane effortlessly taking to the sky as if it was the most, natural, matter-of-fact occurrence in the world. Determinate looked on in silent appreciation, this was incredible! Phenomenal even! Caught up in the rush of that moment, a thought crossed his mind, could *this* be where he came from? Was this the world where he belonged?

A gasp nearby tore Determinate from his gleeful haze. "Call the major!" shouted one of the people in uniform, "the train that has been missing for over 200 years, has been found!" It was like a trigger, the way the building immediately erupted into exuberant conversations. Whether from joyful excitement, or from the irony of this happening just when he had started wondering about his origin, he felt worried.

Determinate felt a sense of warmth spreading through him; they had been looking for him. Not only did he belong somewhere, but he was missed. The pleasant warmth emanated through his carriages, so much so that he was startled by the uncomfortable shuffling of an overheating Alexander. Determinate had forgotten the teen was there, and he regulated the temperature of the carriages to make sure Alexander wasn't baked in the little tool cabinet. When Alexander was comfortable enough, Determinate's attention wavered again. He was swept away by thoughts of how he had somehow, by some stroke of luck, made it back home, yet he felt like a stranger in this unfamiliar world. Then Determinate was yanked out of his own thoughts by a growing commotion around him. He was surrounded by people running towards him, brandishing what looked like weapons, books, and other computer-like objects. *'Okay, so maybe home was a particularly strong word for this environment,'* Determinate thought fearfully, this seemed more like what he imagined the dreaded labs to be like.

As if this whole occurrence was simply part of a choreography sequence, the people surrounding Determinate seemed to seamlessly slip into two separate groups; and the sounds of chatter dimmed to hushed whispers and then silence. The divide naturally created a clear path in front of a rather tall and stocky looking individual, who was flanked by two equally daunting-looking individuals. The man at the front of the arrow formation exuded confidence; an air of dominance seemed to ooze from his pores. He clearly commanded the room, and Determinate had his full attention. Under such an intense gaze it was difficult for the train to avoid feeling intimidated.

The man made an almost imperceptible movement of his head. The action was so insignificant, it would have gone unnoticed. That is if it hadn't been immediately followed by a hand signal, which was done so swiftly Determinate couldn't catch it, by one of the minions, obviously to dismiss the others. Determinate watched as the other normal people, like robots, did some sort of synchronised response of "Yes, Major!" followed by a bow, before they all swiftly exited. Determinate was left alone with the *Major* and his buddies who all looked like living adverts for a company called "Danger & Co" if there ever was one.

The Major had made sure he was timely in his arrival; this was an urgent and classified situation, not that Determinate was aware of that. He felt the pressure of being under the Major's scrutiny. The man's eyes studied him intensely, while occasionally referring to a clipboard he had been handed by one of his minions, and then returning to scrutinise Determinate. The Major circled him, like a vulture circling its lunch, before suddenly stepping back and, seemingly activating a massive grin. His movements appeared so controlled and calculated, they almost seemed unnatural. Determinate suspected that this was one of the reasons the Major had successfully risen through the military ranks in the first place.

The Major clapped his hands, while loudly declaring, "This is the train alright! It must have disappeared through the light vortex all those years ago, just as we had guessed."

Determinate had only encountered the concept of a vortex from the pages of science fiction books, it was slightly amusing to see this token tough guy character seriously mentioning such a thing as a reality. At this point, Determinate felt he was watching some sort of well-executed movie scene, as the Major effortlessly pivoted around to face his equally proud grinning minions,

"We have been trying to discover this vortex for hundreds of years!" he bellowed. "Let's keep this train here, run some tests and get me all the information you can about its condition. Then get the train on the track and keep running it, which may lead us to the whereabouts of the light vortex. Also get this old train modified to our new standard, while you're at it."

The Major didn't bother to turn to face the train again as he walked away, again in an overly controlled-looking manner.

Determinate would have been fascinated to analyse how successfully this Major commanded the area if it weren't for the three words dancing in his mind on a loop *"run some tests."* When he had encountered the concept of a 'stunt double', listening into one of the passenger's conversations, Determinate had thought it to be slightly lazy. Why couldn't the actor simply train for the part? Or why wouldn't the storyline be edited to be within the actor's capabilities? Reviewing his previous stance on the matter, Determinate decided that he had simply been naïve because, at this very moment, he wished that he was just acting and that a brave stunt double was coming to save him from enduring this next part.

He briefly contemplated the idea of escaping, but knowing nothing about this world was a major disadvantage. Even if he did manage to escape out of this giant death trap of a building, who knew what danger lay outside? What if there was no ground for example, and they were in the middle of an ocean somewhere? What if on this planet surrounded by planets, there were giant metal-eating flowers? What if the air closest to the ground was polluted with fatal gases, that would corrode his wheels, ignite his engine, or was just plain toxic to breathe? What if- Determinate stopped himself mid-thought, he was getting carried away. It was becoming ridiculous. He was a train, he didn't breathe! He didn't have any lungs so what exactly was he worrying about?

"*You might not be at risk, but someone else could…*" nudged a small thought in the back of his mind. Alexander! Determinate had completely forgotten about him again. He suddenly became aware of the dull rhythmic thudding from the hidden teen, Alexander was alright for now. The best option for them both was for Determinate to continue to stay perfectly still, at least until he could figure out whether it was safe to attempt an escape. Besides, there was still something off about this whole picture, something was niggling in the back of his mind again, and Determinate desperately wanted to figure it out before they began "modifying" him, whatever that meant, he thought sardonically.

Then he noticed it, as the people spilt back into the area, all of them looked slightly odd. But what in this world didn't? Determinate thought sarcastically. They looked the same strange way in their suits as if they were carrying rucksacks on their backs under their shirts. Determinate hoped that this was just a strange coincidence, that the whole team looked like that from behind. Perhaps in this world that's just how a lot of the population looked. As they started to approach him, Determinate found that, other than the whole hidden rucksack look, they all resembled regular people from the village. This situation was strange to Determinate, watching the observers, as they watched the observed (him). Some of them held clipboards and unpleasant-looking tools, presumably to work on him with. Whilst others seemed to be nothing more than witnesses, judging from their baffled expressions, pointing and hushed comments and whispers. Determinate tried to listen in, to figure out what exactly was the source of their confusion, but his attempts were proving futile, he couldn't understand the language. He had almost given up trying when he finally heard some English, "I've never seen a train this old!" He preferred not knowing what was being said about him.

Determinate was almost too distracted being slightly offended by these strangers acting as if he were *absolutely ancient*, that he nearly missed the most unbelievable scene unfolding in front of him. A cacophony of loud noises filled the air, as the first responder team transformed into horrifying creatures, terrifyingly similar to the one Determinate had seen lurking around in the village. The visceral cracking, tearing and shrieking noises continued as before his very eyes, the creatures multiplied by the dozens. Determinate looked on in horror as some even appeared out of nowhere as if they had been there invisible the whole time. The place was crawling with them, it was like watching an alien infestation. Determinate hoped, for the villagers' sake, that these creatures were not also able to roam around invisibly; how would they be able to defend themselves against a similar invisible infestation?

As lines of people filtered in, Determinate saw some of the creatures assume a position behind some of the more dishevelled, reluctant-looking people that were lagging behind the others. In absolute horror,

Determinate witnessed the creatures violently lashing those men, women, and children back to work. Determinate could almost feel their agony, hearing their pained cries with every crack of the whip. He noticed the ashen faces and sunken eyes of the others; they were so clearly terrified of the creatures. These corrupt monsters were weaponizing their obvious advantages over the people to enslave them. This discovery made the situation at the village significantly more serious than Determinate could ever have anticipated.

Aware of a little shuffle in the tool cabinet, Determinate directed a quiet question to Alexander, "Did you see all of that through the keyhole?"

"Yes! I saw it all," replied a panicked Alexander. "They are going to kill me when they find me here!" he whispered. "Did you see the ones that appeared out of nowhere?!"

"Unfortunately," Determinate responded.

He heard Alexander let out a slightly more forceful worried breath, "Mary and the others don't even know what they're up against! Everyone could be in danger! Imagine how many of them could be hanging about ready to enslave our little village?" he groaned quietly.

Determinate shared the teen's concern, but they had to stay positive. "Let's hope that the A.I.I. team I put together will discover the creature's ability to be invisible somehow before it can become a bigger problem." He paused a little before continuing, "Of course, they will need to work smarter and faster to identify the creature, and study its strengths and weaknesses, to find out how to defeat it before the others find the light vortex."

Determinate was more concerned for Alexander, and the future of the village, than he was for himself at this moment. If these creatures finally found the light vortex that led to their world, all of humanity would be at risk of being trapped and enslaved by these creatures indefinitely, just like the poor people in this world. Since he was already here, Determinate had made up his mind that he would protect Alexander as best as he could, until they could find a way to escape. Meanwhile, he would take every opportunity to observe and learn everything he could to try to help defeat these vile creatures. Suddenly the floor beneath his wheels jolted and he started to move forward.

Determinate hastily scanned the environment again and spotted other people working outside. He noticed what appeared to be a small family, a mother, a father and their children; they were also dishevelled-looking and enslaved to the creatures. Everywhere he looked, Determinate saw discouraged exhausted people, who were powerless to form any sort of impactful resistance team to successfully fight back. They would need a divine miracle to stand a chance!

Continuing to scan, Determinate's eyes settled on another very small family. No one seemed to pay them any attention, not even the creatures. He wondered if it was because of the job they were doing. It seemed like they were out-of-town farmers, travelling in fruit and vegetable wagons. This could be the perfect way to get Alexander off the train. He looked around to find the safest way to get him off the train into the wagons. From what he could see it might be Alexander's best option, to get into the fruit and vegetable wagons not too far from the side door. They had to be strategic with this plan, like moving a chess piece, to get Alexander introduced into that family somehow. Once Alexander was successfully integrated into the community, he would have the opportunity to speak to people and gather more information from them. And at least when the family came here, he and Alexander would have a chance to speak and continue planning, if only for a brief moment.

If this plan worked, they would have a better chance of successfully planning a way back to their world. Determinate had noted that he was moving and pausing at regular intervals, which left Alexander a 2-minute window to do this. They quickly discussed the plan, Alexander agreed that this was the only option to keep him safe right now.

Alexander stealthily got off the train and discreetly climbed into the wagon burying himself nearer to the bottom, and covering himself with the smelly vegetable waste contents inside. He rehearsed the impromptu script the train had advised him to say when he approached the family. He would say that he had lost his parents and was in need of a place to stay. He would negotiate this by offering to work on the field as a means to pay his debt.

As Determinate was moved around, he strained to watch the wagon as far as his vision would let him; he watched relieved as it got to a safe distance on its way out of the city. A part of Determinate was afraid, caught up in worrying thoughts like what if he was wrong about that family? Then wouldn't Alexander be turned over to the creatures? Without a doubt he would definitely be enslaved, but would he be interrogated? What would that even entail? Determinate didn't want to think about it, he reminded himself to keep positive, he could only hope that fate would rest on their side.

Not too long after the cart had set in motion, Alexander felt relieved that it had finally manoeuvred past the cobblestones causing him to be jolted around in his hiding place, and onto a less bumpy terrain. Along with the transition to a quieter environment, Alexander theorised that they had finally departed the city. '*So far, so good*' he thought, the rushed plan was actually working! Perhaps hiding under the nauseating smell of rotten garbage would be worth it after all.

The wagon came to an abrupt stop, flinging Alexander to one end of the cart. He wracked his mind, trying to recall the last couple of seconds to see if he could figure out why they had stopped like that. Suddenly he heard a man's voice utter what sounded like a 3-word command. The family had been chatting away the whole time, in whatever language it was, at times with slightly raised voices or more tense tones, as they presumedly discussed their points. Whatever had triggered this abrupt stop, Alexander wouldn't be able to figure it out, without more information. He contemplated slowly trying to raise his head for a peek outside to see what had caused it, but then he thought about how the cart wasn't exactly overflowing with contents to keep him covered enough to peer over the edge, he could only hope that they had stopped because of something outside that he couldn't see.

Alexander lay there terrified. He didn't move a muscle. Who would have known that all those years of playing statues and being stuck in the mud, his childhood borderline obsession had just been training him for this very second? This was just a very tense game of statues, he convinced himself, willing himself to be as still as humanly possible in this cold, damp, dark, and frankly gross environment. Alexander kept his eyes firmly closed, not just for practicality, but to help him deter the more nerve-wracking fears of getting caught and dying here. The uncertainty of not knowing what was happening from one minute to the next did nothing to help his fight to stay positive and hopeful.

Suddenly, a vice-like grip clamped around Alexander's bicep, wrenching him out of a space of relative safety, into the open. The only reason Alexander was able to distinguish this as a freakishly strong rough worker's hand, as opposed to a demolition tractor's machinery for example, was because of the heat emanating from the hand. Alexander barely had time to catch a breath before he was thrown backwards, slamming into the cart's contents with a sickening squelching sound. As he lay on his back, he watched as a large cloud zipped across the sky, at what seemed like 50 miles an hour. The mix of fear, adrenaline, and disorientation left Alexander feeling as if he had just had an out-of-body experience. In fact, he still wasn't sure that his soul hadn't briefly left his body just a moment ago. Alexander's eyes widened and he gasped, his lungs had been screaming for breath, to replace what had just been knocked straight out of them. Caught up in the moment, he had practically forgotten that breathing wasn't exactly an optional activity, that you could freely choose to do, or not.

Blinking a few times, he tried to orient himself. His mind was still catching up, he was sure of it because he was still hallucinating the clouds zipping across the sky as if they were part of a sports day racing event. *'I don't think that's a hallucination buddy'* a small voice interjected in the back of his mind. Not wanting to confront that thought, he focused his efforts on acknowledging the immediate environment. The family surrounded the wagon, peering down at his form frowning with stern expressions. They spoke to him in gibberish, but something told Alexander they weren't all too pleased to have found him there. He guessed, from the intonation at the end of their sentences, that they had probably been demanding an explanation of some sort from him. After a while, the barrage of questions ceased and they became silent, they stared at him intently and expectedly.

He nearly flinched as the mother moved slightly to put her hands on her hips, whilst she waited. He was relieved that the woman hadn't been pulling out some sort of weapon to harm him, that she instead was simply adopting the motherly interrogation stance that his mum always did when he got into trouble. *'Mum'* he thought with a pang of sadness, she was probably beside herself with worry right now. *'How long had he been missing now? When would he even see her again?* The father's irritated shuffle brought him back to reality, where the family still stood waiting, for him to speak, he assumed. He drew in a scared breath and with a trembling voice he began reciting the script, "I have lost my parents and need a place to stay…"

The moment he started to speak, the children's faces scrunched up in confusion, and they looked to their parents for understanding. Alexander panicked; this was going to go down like a lead balloon if they didn't even understand him. Frantically, he too turned to look at the adults, searching for any indication of understanding. Surprisingly, the adults didn't seem as confused. He didn't know if he was imagining it so he could hold onto a semblance of hope, but they looked like they understood him. He watched hoping they couldn't see him trembling, as they looked at one another, before looking back at him. "You are not of this world. Your language is not of this world," said the mother.

"Where have you come from? How did you get here?" the father demanded impatiently.

Alexander didn't even get a chance to answer, before the mother gasped, "This must be the ancient being the parables spoke of millions of years ago!"

Alexander watched as a shocked expression gradually spread across the father's face.

The mother continued, now using her hands animatedly in her excitement,

"That someone will come and help to liberate us from this oppression and they will come from the offspring world that was formed from our mother world. The offspring world was formed from countless collisions between dust particles, asteroids, and other growing planets, that separated parts of this mother world millions of years ago. We are not sure how many of our children are out there waiting to be discovered.

"Some of the elders of our mother world have been captured and put to sleep in the monsters' prison. The monsters are afraid of them, they cannot die. They are the only ones that have ever been able to kill one of their kind."

"Let's take him to the Resistance Leader II (the second), in the Alpha mountains," said the father, "only then can we determine if he truly is the saviour that the ancient parables predicted, with the ability to raise those elders from their forced slumber. Let's take him there, where he will be tested. If he's the one, he might live to save us. However, if he's not, he will certainly be turned over to the monsters."

They were all in agreement. Alexander didn't have a chance to get a word in edgeways. He didn't mind though; he wouldn't have been able to form a coherent sentence if he tried. Just like the children who stood gawking, dumbstruck by their parents' new ability to speak in an unintelligible language, Alexander wore the same expression. '*These people are in way over their heads!*' he thought. At the ripe age of 17, Alexander had a sneaking suspicion that he wouldn't be eligible to use the "ancient" status just yet. On top of that, there was that quick comment, that essentially clued him into the fact that, in the best-case scenario, it was only that he *might live.* MIGHT?! If that was the best-case scenario, he might as well quit while he was ahead.

If that wasn't worrying enough, the children's expressions at the mention of this *"Alpha Mountain,"* had to be the icing on the cake. Their eyes became so wide, Alexander had been genuinely scared, they might pop right out of their heads. For a split second, the younger one had become quite unstable and wobbly all of a sudden. It was Alexander's personal opinion, based on the knowledge he had so far, that he probably had no business getting involved with whatever they were attempting to rope him into. If he had any other feasible options available right now, he would have tried to argue or negotiate, but he was at their mercy.

As they set off again, he tried to make himself comfy in the cart, while staring at the odd sky to distract himself from his own thoughts. He imagined Mary looking up at their sky in their world, just like he was in this world right now.

Meanwhile, back in the other world in the village, the news had spread like wildfire and the entire community was a melting pot of worry, fear and unrest. They had never had a missing person's case to investigate before, that was something they came across in the media, it had never been so close to home! It was proving to be overwhelming for the village to handle.

Alvin, Mary and Johnny were back together in their usual tutoring room, discussing their most recent findings. Johnny had brought in some photos he had found at home, for the team to look through. It was a stack of photos that had been taken at every one of the mayor's annual village parties that had been a staple in the village since the end of the first world war. Johnny hadn't bothered to sieve through the photos beforehand to make sure he was only bringing the most recent, so they seemed to have photos ranging all the way back to the very first event. Johnny's grandfather had been a member of the council and had kept copies of all the photos for prosperity; this foresight would now hopefully mean that they would be able to identify the person Mary had seen.

The annual village parties were always extremely well attended. It was the event of the year and anyone missing would stick out like a sore thumb. Everyone would notice! Not to mention if someone regularly kept missing the annual party, they would become a social pariah, and for a creature that took such great effort to go relatively unnoticed and discreet, it was not a risk they could take. One of these photos had to have captured them.

Whilst the other two carefully looked through the photos, Alvin was lost in thought, staring straight into space.

"Do you know what, Mary?" he asked, still sounding quite distant. "I saw Mr James last week in a big grey coat. And you know, now that I think about it, it looked as if he had a backpack on underneath the coat," he trailed off slightly. Then he added, clearly a bit disgruntled, "But I couldn't get any closer to see more.

Perhaps it's Mr James you saw?" He suggested, looking from Mary to Johnny in turn.

"If we could find a photo with Mr James in it, I could tell you," Mary replied. They continued to look through the photos but this time, with a focus, they were just looking for Mr James.

Five more minutes passed when Johnny snatched up two photos. "Guys, look at this!" he beckoned, bringing Mary and Alvin's attention to the photos.

"That's Mr James," confirmed Alvin. "Is this the man you saw, Mary?"

Nodding her confirmation, Mary continued looking at the photo.

"Did you know Mr James, Johnny? You picked him out so quickly!" Alvin commented in a semi-accusatory tone. Alvin and Mary both looked at Johnny expectantly. Their expressions morphed from curious to confused, as the boy shook his head and replied,

"No."

"*No?*" Mary mocked, scoffing at the audacity of this kid, attempting such an unbelievable lie. "Well, enlighten me then, dear Johnny boy," said Mary slyly, "exactly how did you find Mr James so quickly? Humour me," she smirked, twirling a lock of her hair.

Johnny looked less than impressed. "Are you calling me a liar?" he said, not bothering to conceal his annoyance.

"No, we're n-" Alvin was cut short by stern looks from both the arguing parties. Sighing, he put his hands up in surrender and swivelled further into his seat. He would leave the young people to squabble amongst themselves; he didn't need telling twice!

As undeterred as ever Mary shrugged, "Just explain!" she snapped sassily.

Johnny gave each of them angry pointed stares, muttering, "I expect it from her, not you," as he made eye contact with Alvin. This boy was many decades his junior, but Alvin felt like he had just been scolded; he resisted the urge to make it known by squirming in his seat though.

"'Her' has a name," snapped Mary.

Johnny rolled his eyes and stuck his tongue out at her. Alvin tried not to worry about the squabble. It was a stressful time for everyone; maybe for the youngsters, these little arguments were how they managed that stress.

"No, I have not seen this man before," Johnny reiterated, emphasising every word and again fixing them with pointed stares. "Hasn't either of you noticed that he looks exactly the same in both pictures?" He paused waiting for them to catch up with his realisation. Then at the vague expressions on his elders' faces, Johnny huffed, shaking his head in disappointment. "The problem is, this picture was taken in 2001," he moved his finger to point at the other photo, "but this one was taken in 1944."

The other two sat up straighter, studying the photos in greater detail. It appeared that in the 57 years between the photos, Mr James had managed to keep his physical appearance and even his clothing in exactly the same condition.

"Oh my God!" gasped Alvin. "You're actually right!"

Now it was Johnny who wore the smirk. He looked directly at Mary with his arms crossed and a satisfied expression, wiggling his eyebrows mockingly. Mary glared quickly but said nothing. Knowing he had won Johnny beamed his cheekiest grin.

Alvin, who had missed that entire interaction, being completely absorbed in studying the photos, suddenly huffed in irritation, "I really hope he isn't the creature."

"Why?" asked Mary. In an ideal world, no one would want to discover anyone in their community to be a terrifying, dangerous creature, sure. But they *did* live in the real world, so unfortunately the whole point of their search so far had been to identify the creature. It sounded like Alvin had some other reasons on his mind, causing him to have these reservations.

"Because if he is, we are in a lot more trouble than we imagined. James is a very important government official, armed with power and police protection. He's the head manager of the village council with major influence in all the other towns nearby too. We'll never be able to get to him, let alone stop him," Alvin explained, shaking his head.

"Just watch me!" Mary said with vehemence. "I'm afraid of nothing! And no one! I will go to the end of the entire universe to find my Alexander!"

Caught up in her own impassioned outburst, Mary waved her fist in the air furiously, as if she were face-to-face and trying to intimidate her opponent. The fact that she completely missed the sceptical look Johnny had given her, right before he had choked with laughter at her impromptu performance, just went to show how absorbed she was in whatever she was thinking about. Or *whoever…*

Mary ran her hands through her hair nervously, as she began sorting through her mind's jumbled thoughts out loud. At this point, Alvin and Johnny just watched in silence munching on some snacks as Mary began pacing the room and voicing her thoughts indirectly. "Well, everything and everyone has a weakness," she paused to turn around to continue pacing the other way. "We just need to follow him long enough to figure out what it is." Mary nodded silently, egging herself on. "If he's our guy, and we find out what his weaknesses are, that will be our chance to strike the creature where it hurts, and win."

Alvin and Johnny began nodding fervently in agreement. Johnny hated to admit it, but she had made a valid point and suggested a very logical and achievable plan after all. "Let's start tomorrow morning," he suggested. "Mum and I will be out grocery shopping anyway, so I can keep an eye out at the supermarkets."

"I can monitor his whereabouts during the days," Mary offered.

Alvin nodded in approval; the situation didn't feel so hopeless with a plan coming together so nicely. "Then I'll keep a lookout at night," he said. "I forgot to tell you I have already invited my ex-soldier friend to come on board with us. I'll be picking him up at the airport tomorrow morning. We've arranged that he will be staying with me."

As they sat there planning and encouraging one another, the team were completely oblivious to the reality that somewhere out there, in another world, Determinate and Alexander were desperately wondering how they could get back to them. Or, failing that, how they could find a way to get a warning message to the team, that there was an army of creatures out there, looking for a way to invade and overthrow their world?

Travelling along the road in the wagon, Alexander kept noticing most things seemed to be in the patterns of 3, 6 and 9. Although he couldn't quite figure out the full significance of that in this confusing world, he did remember being taught, back in his world, about a philosopher and inventor called Nikola Tesla, who believed that these three numbers might be the key to the universe. Alexander had hated having to write several points arguing persuasively for and against the validity of Tesla's theory as homework, especially since this was just pre-work for a class debate.

In fact, it was because he had been so irritable and reluctant to do the homework that Mary had decided to help him in exchange for snacks. They had spent that afternoon scoffing and giggling, or perhaps it should be said that Alexander had spent the afternoon giggling at moody Mary's befuddled expressions, as she scoffed and guffawed at the theory. A small hint of a smile broke across Alexander's face; it had been safe to say that Mary remained unconvinced. She had been firmly on the 'against' side of the argument.

Alexander had to admit, Tesla's arguments had sounded a bit far-fetched. It wasn't really easy to wrap your head around and get completely on board with a theory that came from the same mind of a man from 'ye olden days', who also spoke about having had an out-of-body experience as a child, which had transferred him into "new places and cities" he had never seen before. But that was what Alexander had thought *before* discovering just a few new things, *like the fact that some trains could talk, or discovering alternate universes, and giant shape-shifting creatures who wanted to invade and conquer Earth!* Alexander shook his head to pause his racing thoughts. Now, he couldn't help but allow himself to wonder, was it even the slightest bit possible that Tesla could have come to this place? Or that the people here could have somehow visited him? Is this where it all began? Did life originate from here?

All potentially lethal dangers aside, the scenery was breathtaking. Alexander entertained the thought of Mary shooting him a quick jealous glare that she had missed out on it all. The road was lined on either side by distant green mountains and forests with so many different colours, it was as if the forests had been ambushed in a massive paintball game. As he looked closer, Alexander realised that even this seemed to abide by the same unwritten rule (*well he assumed it was unwritten anyway*). The randomly coloured forests weren't completely random. As abstract as they seemed at a glance, the clusters either appeared to be splattered with foliage of three different colours, six different colours, or nine. Again, the pattern of 3, 6 and 9. If he found a way out of here and back home, would he be like a modern-day Tesla with people wondering whether he was randomly obsessed with those numbers?

As Alexander got closer and closer to the small city that had previously been in the distance, it was harder to ignore the nerve-wracking feeling, overriding all his best efforts to distract himself from worrying about what they were going to do to him. He squinted at the closest splattered trees, and somehow Alexander was surprised that neither the trees nor the fruit on them was known or even recognisable to him. Out of the corner of his eye, Alexander was drawn to movement. He watched intrigued as rivers flowed all around him, navigating seamlessly in diverse directions as if they were able to communicate and signal where they were headed so they could avoid a collision. Was the "*water*" communicating? Could it be, that in this world even water was sentient, like the train? *How on earth would that even work?* Alexander pondered. Was the "water" even water?! he thought. Alexander didn't know, but one thing was sure, he certainly would not be the cat that got done in by curiosity on this occasion! Someone else could test that theory!

As the wagon travelled further, he could see a family gazing into the far distance towards the right. He was very curious to see what they were looking at, and when his gaze followed theirs, a bright glint caught his eye. He flinched quickly, shutting his eyes whilst turning his head and bringing his arm up to shield his eyes instinctively. When his eyes had adjusted, Alexander could see that the light was being reflected off the bark of the trees, As if everything else hadn't already been new and disorientating enough, somehow light was being refracted off the tree bark casting a rainbow-like light from a distance.

This place made no logical sense to Alexander. He just couldn't wrap his mind around any of it at all. In fact, the only reasonable explanation he could think of was that he had to be dreaming.

"Ouch," he hissed through clenched teeth, quickly rubbing the spot on his arm that he had just impulsively pinched. At least now he could rule out the idea that he was dreaming. *More like nightmare-ing*, the little voice in the back of his head groaned. Squashing another wave of panic that had been threatening to surge up, Alexander willed himself to think harder. There *had* to be a reasonable explanation for all of this. It was the most beautiful, confusing place he had ever seen (you know, minus all the deadly parts).

He wracked his brain trying to conjure up an acceptable explanation. Perhaps he had been in some sort of near-death experience, an accident and this was a hallucination of another life beyond death, and what that could be! As soon as he thought it, his face scrunched up. He didn't believe that. He couldn't. That would mean that after death, humans were just destined to be enslaved by aliens. That was not on!

He felt the sickening wave arise again, was he already dead? *More like, about to* die! The little voice unhelpfully reminded him. Alexander's heart rate picked up, with the wave of worry surging triumphantly over his efforts to quash it. Maybe this would be the end of him, *"I haven't even lived life yet!"* whined his inner voice. He had never even gotten to say goodbye to his parents! In fact, there were lots of things he hadn't gotten to experience yet. He hadn't invented something ground-breaking that made him a millionaire or earned him a Nobel prize, he had never finished college, celebrated with that perfect dance at prom with the prettiest girl in school. If his life ended this way, it would be like a tragic version of that old cringey Chickflick Mary had made him watch, called 'Never Been Kissed'. But in this version, he would just die never having kissed a girl. Well, a very specific moody girl. Alexander grimaced, there were also other random things he had kind of always wanted to do, like attend a fancy ballroom dance, not that he would ever admit that out loud. He didn't have a mirror with him right now, but Alexander was sure that the sour expression on his face screamed the words 'doom' and 'gloom'; he hadn't done anything he wanted to do in his life before it came to an end.

Eventually, it was his rumbling stomach that distracted Alexander from his spiralling thoughts. Who would have known that worry and confusion could work up such an appetite? "I'm starving," he thought.

He scanned the area desperately, looking around to find anything that looked remotely palatable. It would be a risk, sure, but it was one he was willing to take. His eyes landed on some sorry-looking stray leaves, some of them wilting and moulding to take on the shapes of the other unwanted bits and pieces thrown onto the bottom of the wagon. Would they notice if he started to eat these leftover leaves? Would they care? Alexander shrugged, reaching for the top ones that looked the '*freshest*,' they were discarded after all. As soon as the leaf hit his taste buds, he gagged. Every bite sent shivers of revolt and objection through his body. It didn't even get better once it was in his stomach, a safe taste-free distance away from his horrified taste buds; it felt alien and ill-fitting in his stomach, but he had to keep going. He could only hope through clenched teeth that he would be able to digest it. If he was going out, Alexander had no intention of going out as a hungry man.

As they drew nearer to the entrance of the city, Alexander could see other people making their way there in a disciplined fashion. An eerie silence hung over them like a thick, sticky treacle coating of nothing but blind acceptance of their abysmal fate. Alexander couldn't make out even one person who didn't look absolutely dejected. It was like the natural instinct to resist, fight or defend themselves had been drained out of all of them. Alexander shuddered, suddenly wishing he had not seen so many dystopian zombie apocalypse-themed movies. It was hard for him not to associate these people with the mindless zombie characters that were often featured on their screens at home.

Suddenly, without so much as a peep, Alexander witnessed the line of individuals seamlessly begin to shift to the side of the road. It looked as if they were making way for something they already knew was coming. But Alexander was confused, he hadn't heard anything. Not a beep, horn, bell or some road rage-fuelled shout to make way. Against his better judgement, Alexander peered curiously behind him and was again confused. There wasn't anyone or anything behind them. Nothing that he could see anyway. His heart sank a little bit because only two possible reasons for this came to mind, and neither of them left Alexander comfortable. On one hand, it could be that some invisible horrific creature was just tagging along casually behind them; or potentially worse (depends how you see it) they were clearing a path for him!

No. Way. Alexander shook his head. That wasn't possible. It wasn't that he preferred the idea of being tailed by a giant invisible creature, he just couldn't figure out how this could be. Not only did he hear nothing, but there had been no discussions about him and no audible instructions to move to the side to let them through. Alexander didn't see anything resembling a communication device, which could have been used to contact anybody, to let them know that they- well, *he* was there.

Alexander's sense of trepidation grew as they passed all the others. He was being transported to what appeared to be some sort of temple that seemed to be made from some precious stones. Although he wasn't given much time to gawk at the magnificent building, from what he could see, the stone appeared to incorporate what he could only assume to be particles of crystal, gold and silver. It seemed that these elements weren't just embedded into the stone for the opulence, but it looked as if the stone component itself naturally contained them. If Mary was here now, he would even sacrifice two whole Jammie Dodgers to bet her that the stone naturally occurred like that. "*Well, as far as anything here could be considered natural anyway,*" thought Alexander to himself. On second thought, Alexander wasn't sure that the bet was worth giving up two Jammy Dodgers. That was a wholly unnatural thought, what was he thinking? The atmosphere of this world must have been getting to him because that thought was plain crazy!

As if to distract him from his impending spiral into the mind of a madman, with ridiculous ideas like willingly giving Mary two of his Jammie Dodgers, whispers erupted all around him. It had started as one or two hushed whispers, and then a murmur, and it had grown louder and louder until it sounded like a wall of whispers surrounding him. It was impossible to distinguish one conversation from another, but Alexander had been too busy wishing he had some Jammy Dodgers to notice the whispers right away. Slowly, he peeked over the top of the wagon, peering around at the owners of voices, he saw that he was surrounded, all eyes were trained on him, it was unnerving. Even more unsettling was the fact that even though Alexander was looking right at them, he realised he still couldn't decipher a word they were saying.

Alexander assumed he looked a bit comical, peeping over the top of the wagon, his eyes going to and fro, scanning the crowd to find anyone whispering anything he could understand. It didn't help him at all; he had no idea what they were saying. So, he grappled with trying to read the room. They seemed to be a mixed crowd. Whilst the majority of them appeared understandably wary of him, they still looked relatively comfortable and approachable. Others stood tense as if all their muscles were coiled and ready to pounce on him at any given moment, should he even think about making a wrong step. *Whatever could be considered a wrong step in this place anyway.* Just a few moments ago, he had thought these people looked lifeless, now he felt himself shrink back slightly under some of their harsh gazes.

The roaring of the whispers subsided suddenly. Alexander again felt out of step, having no idea what triggered these changes. He was annoyed with himself, here he was, potentially about to die and he was essentially sulking about being left out…

"*Get a grip mate*!" Alexander chided himself, in his thoughts.

"Is it true?"

"That puny thing? Don't be ridiculous!"

"Don't say that."

"Maybe it's the one from the prophecy?"

"Do you think he might be the hero that has come to save us?"

"Is he the one?"

Again, Alexander felt blindsided, the atmosphere here was really messing with his mind. How was he suddenly able to understand them as if they were speaking English? The wagon jolted forward, moving Alexander slowly through the crowd. Somehow, the physical motion seemed to be helping him process what he had just heard.

They were debating if he were some sort of superhero to save them. Oh, great.

Now, the tension and resistance in the atmosphere made a little bit more sense. The unmistakable sense of rebellion electrified the air. Alexander thought it was ironic that the people who happened to share his doubts were the same ones putting him on edge. It was clear to see that they weren't too keen on buying into this ideology. It was also clear for anyone to see that they struggled to believe that he could be the leader they had been waiting for to save them. He didn't blame them; he felt the exact same way. What would happen when they realised that he wasn't the one they were looking for? He hoped to heaven that they would at least consider sparing his life.

Amidst the terror, Alexander felt he could hear his mother's voice repeating one of her favourite sayings, "It's not what I wish to be, nor where I wish to go; but the universe will always choose for us." He had always hated the saying. Firstly, because he had heard it so often, and secondly, it sounded a lot like, "Oh, well, let's just give up," to him. He didn't want the universe to choose for him this time. For once he wanted to choose for himself, and his choice would be - not to be here.

His mother had always been more of a 'go with the flow' type of person. She would often stare at him bewildered at how 'spirited' he was. She would always gasp, "I've no idea where you get it from, son. Not from me, that's for sure!" while staring at him wide-eyed as if he had four heads, whenever he would take matters into his own hands and steer his life in the direction he wanted to go. Alexander had believed, for as long as he could remember, that everyone could at least exercise some influence on how their life progressed. He had never just gone with the flow when it wasn't headed in the direction he wanted to go in, and he certainly wouldn't be starting now.

It was time to pull his socks up and switch his brain on. He would have to be alert and keep his wits about him if he were ever going to get back to his world.

"How did he get here?" someone shouted.

"Where did he come from?" came another voice, the crowd was getting restless.

"Put him with the others in the cave prison," demanded a voice from the back.

Then came a suggestion that everyone agreed on, "Take him to the chamber of trials; in there, no one can lie, and everything will be revealed."

A chorus of agreement flooded the crowd and then Alexander found himself once again on the move. He guessed they were taking him to the 'chamber of trials' and he would soon find out what that was all about.

He had barely caught his breath when the onslaught of questions began. He realised that he was being interrogated and wondered when it would all end. It felt like hours had passed when Alexander concluded that they were, in fact, trying to kill him… with boredom.

"I'm asking you for the final time, where did you come from?"

Alexander had half a mind to start his answer with '*And for the last time, I'm answering…*', but he settled on playing it safe, "I don't know," he replied.

"How did you get there?"

"I don't know," Alexander replied again in a monotone.

His interrogator must have sensed his frustration. He sighed, "We were expecting the miracle to come in some spectacular fashion, like fly down from the sky to save the day, not just a strange regular person who appeared out of nowhere." Alexander nodded hesitantly, what was he supposed to do with that information?

"Traveller-"

"Alexander," he interrupted, correcting his interrogator, earning him a disapproving glance. He shuffled his feet, looking down at the ground sheepishly.

He was still looking down when something unexpectedly flew towards him, knocking him straight off his feet in surprise. For a second, Alexander just stared at the roof. There wasn't a mirror there, but he was sure that his facial expression had changed. He groaned, thinking of how embarrassing it was that the *"hero"* had just fallen flat on his back because of-, well, he had no idea what even hit him. He craned his neck all around to find the culprit. Alexander had never had to try so hard not to facepalm - a piece of material. He had been knocked onto his back by a piece of flimsy material, in front of a live audience of people who already had very little faith in his abilities. Could he just disappear?

He was sort of relieved when the interrogator just kept going, he could pretend the attention wasn't completely on him. "Change into that, and walk through the middle of the rocks, the path will reveal itself to you with each step you take," he instructed.

Was he in some sort of Indiana Jones movie?

Before he knew it, Alexander was approaching the rocks, which they told him were debris remnants fallen from an asteroid. As he looked at the rock, he wondered what exactly asteroids looked like here, because up close, the rocks looked more like a ragged three-dimensional mirror. Except, like everything else here, it was even more strange - like a mirror, but with ulterior properties. Unlike a normal mirror which would reflect a person's own image back to them, this mirror rock wasn't reflecting Alexander at all, it was showing his innermost thoughts. Or maybe it was just a collection of random images because not all the images were things Alexander had been thinking about or recognised.

There was one image, which seemed to transfix all his attention. It was so unfamiliar, but he couldn't avert his eyes. In fact, Alexander wasn't quite sure if that half-wilted leaf had finally reached his brain, causing him to hallucinate. It appeared that it was getting larger, occupying the whole rock surface. What was this image about?

A few gasps behind him reassured him that he wasn't suffering from an alien leaf-induced hallucination, and for that he was relieved. Glancing back at the crowd of people, he saw their eyes were stuck on the rock.

"Look what the mirror sees in him," a voice commented, in disbelief.

Alexander resisted the urge to shout and begin frantically looking around for hidden cameras. The alien rock was reflecting what *it saw* in him. Alexander ruffled the back of his hair, trying to dislodge the growing irritation at the constant nonsensical surprises on this planet. He had to get home. Soon.

He felt unnerved, here he was in a ridiculous loincloth, about to walk on a path that, if he understood correctly, wasn't necessarily there, while surrounded by a crowd of onlookers on an alien planet. If this was a movie, he was watching… *on the couch with popcorn… and Mary-*

"Focus Alexander, focus!" he thought, redirecting his straying line of thoughts. He glanced back at the crowd, unsure of himself. Most people's attention was still strictly trained on the reflection, but his interrogator, whom Alexander guessed was the leader, met his gaze. He gestured Alexander forward, ushering him to continue… to wherever Alexander was supposed to be going. He could be walking straight into the stomach of some man-eating creature for all he knew.

He took a deep breath and a tentative step forward, then froze, one foot on the path and the other one back where he knew the ground was safe. Before his very eyes, the rocks began to transform, morphing and surging upright to form a smooth, straight line. Alexander didn't have a ruler, but he had no doubt it was completely straight. It didn't just change shape, it also changed colour, now resembling a mature white crystal stalagmite, with strips and glints of silver woven in and shimmering through.

There was an unrecognisable and odd melody emanating from the rock as Alexander proceeded along the materialising pathway. He felt strangely comforted by the new onslaught of hushed murmurs. It meant that he wasn't the only one not entirely sure of what was going on or what, if anything, this strange melody meant. Glancing over his shoulder, he noticed everyone looking around to whichever elder was closest to them, to find out if they understood what the incomprehensible sound of this other language meant, but they were met with blank stares and shrugged shoulders. It was clear that although no one appeared to understand it, it managed to command everyone's attention; everyone seemed to stand still showing some sort of reverence to this entity.

Three rocks were aligned in a row on either side of Alexander. As he moved to step forward, more steps popped up aligning his path. Alexander had always been a very practical guy, he liked to have all the information before making decisions. So naturally, he was less than impressed overhearing the crowd discussing that he would either vanish *like the others* who falsely claimed to be the hero sent to deliver them or finally, he would be the one to transform into something else and save them. '*Was there even a positive outcome in those potentials?*' He thought, *'and just how many people had vanished before?'* So many questions; he really wished this had been discussed before he started walking a more elaborate version of the plank.

A part of him must have known that there was no point attempting to turn back, who knew what risks that would pose? So, whilst his mind had drifted off on several tangents, Alexander's feet had carried him along to the end of the path. Suddenly, he felt like he stood there, in full armour, warrior-like, armed with some sort of tough stoney object in his right hand. Looking at it, he noted how it looked like marble with lots of different coloured slivers running through it. It wasn't just the sudden materialisation of the clothes and accessories that he couldn't explain, it was the way he felt oddly disconnected from himself as if his body had also changed and become somewhat unfamiliar.

He shut his eyes, clenched his teeth and released the small burst of tense air he had been holding, hoping that he was just in an especially hyper-aware state, because he could swear that he was feeling bulky. It was as if he had been working out for years, building muscles he never knew he had! He half cracked open an eye… *and yep*, his whole body had been transformed. Alexander grimaced; he looked like every token gym instructor advert ever; definitely not his style.

He was still feeling a little off when he began to suspect that his transformation was still happening. What used to sound like nonsensical babbling to his ears, was now starting to make sense. Alexander understood all the languages. In fact, he felt confident he would be able to communicate with little difficulty. The rate of drastic changes on this planet was giving him whiplash.

"Alexander," a woman's voice called.

He looked up, scanning the crowd of faces to find the source of the voice. There were a few eyes on him, but as far as his lip-reading abilities could go, he didn't see anyone speaking to him. Confused, he scanned his surroundings once again. It took another confused minute before he sensed it, someone's eyes on him.

"Whoa, whoa, you're about to look away from me," warned the voice.

There were only three women where he had been looking and only one of them looked his way. They made eye contact. "Bingo," the woman confirmed. Alexander cocked his head to the side. He had heard the woman's voice clear as day, but she hadn't *said* anything. He could have sworn her mouth hadn't moved at all. 'S*he must have a degree in ventriloquism,*' he thought to himself.

"I'm going to disregard whatever you just accused me of, in good faith that it wasn't disrespectful," came the voice again, while the woman, with one raised eyebrow, fixed him with a pointed look.

'Yep, her mouth definitely didn't move,' he thought. The singing rocks had changed his clothes, body, and brain and given him the ability to hear people's thoughts. Alexander couldn't help but grin, he had to admit it was kind of cool to be a mind reader! He could just imagine how much easier it would make his life; he could read Mary's mind and find out why she was mad at him. Or he could find out the perfect gift for her birthday. Life would be GREAT! '*I miss my magpie,*' Alexander thought, morosely. The woman's puzzled expression signalled the creeping invasion growing across his cheeks. This lack of privacy was going to take some getting used to.

"Did magpies disappear from your world too?" the woman asked, shocked.

It was Alexander's turn to look confused. "No…? Are magpies extinct here?" he asked hesitantly. He had no idea where this conversation was going.

"Unfortunately, yes. But it was inevitable that this would happen since it was such a delicacy here. Calm down, young man," the ventriloquist lady chastised abruptly, making Alexander aware of the fact that his eyes were nearly falling out of their sockets. The thought of anyone eagerly digging into some Kentucky Fried Magpie frankly made him nauseous.

He looked away bashfully, landing his gaze right into the eye line of another burlier person.

"Great, we need a hero and the universe sent… a child," the less than impressed man scowled looking him up and down disdainfully. "We're all doomed," mister Burly-guy thought before quickly assuming a neutral facial expression.

Alexander winced at the man's obvious lack of faith in him even though, glancing aside, he was again granted unwanted insight into yet another mind. '*Note to self*', thought Alexander, '*I can read everyone's mind that I look at.*' He realised that he was out of his depth here, he could hear the thoughts of others and he knew the lady could hear his thoughts, but could everyone else? He decided it was probably safest to keep quiet about that little fact.

"Alexander," one of the elders called out catching his attention. He turned and looked straight over at her. The elder continued, "This is your final question; what day, month, and year you were born?"

"June 3rd 1999," he replied automatically. He recalled fondly how his mother always used to feel compelled to mention that he had been born on the day that felt for her as the longest of the year. Yet another wave of chatter bubbled up, but this time it sounded more upbeat.

"Boy! Do you understand what this number means at all? How significant the numbers are?!" another elder exclaimed.

"No," replied Alexander, shaking his head.

"These numbers are a part of the keys to the Universe!"

It took a moment for Alexander to follow the drift, it was the 3, 6, 9 pattern all over again.

"And," continued the elder, "you are the sixth person to walk through those rocks that have received confirmation of their number. You are the bridge between Universes!"

Alexander speculated on whether the old man was in fact senile. How else would he be able to speak so animatedly about something as absurd as that? Alexander willed himself not to forget to ask what happened to the last five people. It was in his best interest that that little point wasn't simply glossed over and forgotten.

The elder continued excitedly, "You will be able to form bridges between our world and the other. Now that you are here, we can find them at last." *'Yep, definitely senile'* Alexander confirmed; but no one was intervening and trying to stop him, so, of course, the old man continued, "Come," he beckoned," we have much to do and not enough time to do it."

He was surprisingly agile for an elderly man, Alexander had to break into a jog to keep up with him. When Alexander had finally caught up with him, he found himself matching the old man's stride. The elder nodded in acknowledgement of him, "From now on your training in patience, wisdom, knowledge, understanding and combat will start. We'll let you rest for the remainder of the day, and we will start in the morning, at the sound of the first bird's song."

The knot in his stomach tightened, it was as if he had bitten off more than he could chew, except he hadn't "bitten" at all, he was being force-fed.

***

Meanwhile, back in Alexander's home village, the feeling of sorrow, tension, terror and anger interwoven through the air was palpable. It was so tightly woven it felt like every movement, every closed door caused an injury. Grief burned and cut like a brush against a taut rope. Why did it feel like they were no closer to finding Alexander? The frustration and unrest grew unchecked amongst the team, Alexander's parents and the community. Everyone knew about the situation, it had become a national investigation, carried out by several government agencies.

Many were still reeling from the shocking discoveries that emerged from the news reaching other parts of the world. According to the global defence security agency, they had been having similar inexplicable cases of missing people, planes and ships for many years.

Members of the military had been commissioned to visit their little village. They came to meet local law enforcement officers, to work together with the town's General who oversaw the investigation. The military had come to Mary's house with the local police at first light. Mary recalled gruffly how the rascals had practically abducted her family from their house one by one, saying that they just wanted to ask them some questions. *"I mean honestly,"* thought Mary grimly, *"they didn't even have the decency to wait for a more respectable time."*

They had been escorted into a waiting area, with the door closed behind them… from the outside. "Why are they locking us in?" Mary glowered. "Are they just expecting us to sit on these rusty stinking metal chairs?" she asked, half-heartedly kicking at one of the unsuspecting chair legs. It wasn't too long before the rascals came back and moved Mary to another room, with some familiar faces. Then they locked them in just like that and plodded off again. A few hours crawled by with nothing. Not a whisper of a question. They had just been left there to twiddle their thumbs.

Mary's mood spread like a contagion; everyone was fed up. Grumpy Alvin snapped first. He marched straight up to the door bashing it and shouting, "What's going on? Let us out of here! Let us out of here! Give me some water, or something, for goodness's sake!"

Little Johnny was very focused and told them, "Guys, do not tell them about Determinate and our investigation until we know whom to trust."

Minutes later they started calling them to enter three different rooms to be questioned. The questioning went on for over 60 minutes, all about the last time they had seen Alexander and the train and they kept repeating the same questions over and over. Then they were sent back to another waiting area where the General's team had briefed them on the outcome of the questioning, instructing the team to stay away from the official investigation and to no longer be involved in any activities on their own and what would happen if the team didn't do as they were told.

"I know you all are very good friends," said the General, "but if you get involved in this investigation, you will be prosecuted."

Mary lost it and shouted, "Arrest me now! Arrest me now! You are very aggressive and rude, you, big bald-headed prick! I am getting involved, like it or not and there is nothing you can do to stop me!" She stormed out of the building, crying. The General asked one of the local police officers to go outside and comfort her.

Mary was really surprised when the officer put her arms around her to comfort her and said, "It's going to be ok, Mary. Ever since they got here, they haven't stopped looking at us as insignificant and ordering us around too. We are all getting frustrated."

At that moment, Mary felt an instant connection between herself and the police officer and thought that some foundation of trust could be built. Or could it be just one of their mind games to get her talking?

Over her shoulder, Mary could see Alvin and little Johnny following her outside too.

"Mary! Mary, are you ok?" said Alvin.

"What's your name?" Mary asked the police officer.

"Call me Rebecca." As Alvin was getting closer, Rebecca said, "Good morning." Alvin was looking at her, like, *should I know you?* Rebecca realised that Alvin couldn't remember her. "It's Rebecca, your past student. I'm Katie's daughter, Katie's last child."

"Rebecca?"

"Yes, I am."

"Child, forgive me, you have grown. So, you have chosen to become a police officer. Why this career?"

"I love to serve and protect people."

Mary asked Alvin, "Do you know each other?" with a jealous look.

"Yes, Mary. I taught all her brothers and sisters in school."

After getting back from the questioning, Little Johnny said, "Guys, do you think we should try and get to know Rebecca more? She might be a good person to ask for help. We have made some progress in tracking some suspicious people but we can't confirm any historical information about them on our own. She could use police resources to help us."

"I don't know," replied Mary, "but I feel some sort of connection with her. I never normally feel this way."

"Like you feel with Alexander?" Little Johnny poked.

"Shut up, you idiot! They should have kept you locked up in the police station."

"Stop it, both of you!" said Alvin. "Let's give it a try and see if she can help us. But listen carefully, we will not give her any information about the train, Alexander or our investigation. Let's just tell her that we are doing a historical study on a family living in this village and where they have come from to settle here."

"That sounds like a good idea!" said Little Johnny.

The next day they compiled a list of suspicious names that they would like to have checked out. Mary took the responsibility to go back to the station to ask for Rebecca. She explained to Rebecca what the team had planned and she was more than happy to help with any educational requirements, after all, it sounded like an important community project.

"Give me a few days to get back to you with the information, because we have a lot going on at the station at the moment."

"Thanks, Rebecca! See you soon," said Mary.

Mary then rushed back to the centre to celebrate breaking down the information barriers. With the other data that they had gathered, the additional information from the police should condense the list and put them in the perfect position to identify all possible suspects.

***

Back in the other universe, the elders helped Alexander to make a necklace with the same marble-type stone that was put in his hand at the end of the trial. He was getting ready to be trained in combat first thing in the morning. All he had been doing for the last 30 days was helping the elderly and children with their everyday routines. He felt that he was ready to move on to the next stage and he realised that the first 30 days had not been wasted. They had tested him for loyalty, honesty, willingness to help others, kindness to everyone and most of all, the love for everyone and the patience he exercised by still helping others even when they didn't deserve it. He saw people of all races living here as one. His speed at learning had increased rapidly since he walked the rock path.

Being with the resistance, Alexander learned their history, culture and to be a person of value rather than fame or success; inequality wasn't a seed in this world. Included in his first test and training was to see if he would treat all people equally. The oneness here was like the ocean: water combined with salt, with no intention to separate them one day. The elders taught Alexander that morning that they didn't believe in a class system. Here, equal opportunity was given to everyone, from the greatest to the least person. There was also one other surprise, religion did not separate the people of this world. The centre of religion here was love for each other.

In all this world's history, segregation amongst the people was not known until the creatures took over. In most parts of the world, sadly, the creature instigated classification where some people were considered more important than others. The segregation seed germinated in their hearts like a General Sherman giant sequoia tree and became a part of them. This venomous disease caused disloyalty, pride, jealousy, greed and selfishness. Whereas before, there were no borders, and no migration issues, due to the same opportunity given to everyone regardless of where they came from, now all that changed since the creatures took over.

Alexander, however, had been lucky enough to escape into the mountain where the resistance lived and maintained the same high values. On top of that, technology here was hundreds of years advanced. Alexander learned that they cured all sicknesses known to mankind. People here did not die from the seven physical causes of illness, only by very old age or a tragic accident. The normal lifespan here was almost one thousand years. "If I could only find a way to get back to the other world, my grandfather wouldn't have been dying of cancer," Alexander thought to himself.

"Boy! Go and help pack the fruit and vegetable wagon!" commanded one of the elders, snapping Alexander out of his thoughts. "Tomorrow, we would like you to travel with the family to the big city, to drop them off and gather information about where they are keeping the leaders asleep. Your entry garment is a CCTV that captures all sound and pictures and transmits instantaneously to our servers here."

Alexander did as he was told and went off to sleep that night, very excited to see Determinate and to update him that he was still alive. His first question would be to find out if there was a plan to get them back home.

Leaving the mountain, the next morning, he noticed that there were no creatures on the way, only from the foot of the mountain to the main city. "Why did we not see a creature on the way here? They only appeared at the base of the mountain," he wondered. "There must be some sort of high energy frequency from the foot of the mountain that they can't sequence with. Only those that manage to escape into the mountain, are allowed to stay there as farmers. They check everyone and everything passing this point. The other travellers said these mountains are made of other planet rocks that landed here millions and millions of years ago, thus this was called a secret mountain. I guess, there are many, many, mysteries to this mountain yet to be discovered. The elders are still studying what the creatures are afraid of in these rocks."

Alexander could see the city getting closer and closer, by all the technology that took to the sky and the types of transportation used on the street. He could see the fear in the people moving about in silence and against their will.

"Stop the cart here! Get out! Let us check what's inside!" shouted one of the guards. "Who is this new one? We have never seen this one before!" said the guard looking straight into Alexander's face demanding an answer in their language. The rest of the travellers could smell death because if Alexander spoke in his own language, they would know that he was not from this world.

When Alexander answered in their dialect, "Sir, I'm from the mountain. I just want to help," the creature gained confidence that he was not a threat.

The relief on the faces of the others was instant, overcoming the fear of death. They still couldn't work out how Alexander could now speak and understand all the languages here. As they passed the checkpoint, he could feel that question coming from the others. And they indeed did ask before Alexander could even finish thinking about it. At this point, he was still not sure if he could trust them so he lied and told them that he was learning slowly from the others during training. He knew that he shouldn't lie because that is not how he was brought up, but he also remembered that if every truth should be spoken, there would be no peace on earth.

There was a rest period given after delivering and storing the food when the farmers could have something to eat, drink and use the restroom before going back. The time given to do all that was just 60 minutes. Alexander knew that he had to find Determinate before they moved on, so he started looking around in the train yard but couldn't see the train anywhere. "Maybe they pulled it apart for investigation," he thought. "I don't know. Maybe Determinate has gone back and left me here. But how could he?" With this worry in mind, Alexander went back to join the others. "I think he has left me behind. What do I do now? I'm all alone," sobbed Alexander.

In the distance, Alexander could see some children sitting down, eating, and just behind them he could see another area where the paint technicians were changing the colour of some trains. Alexander went to have a closer look. He couldn't believe his eyes! He was just in time to identify Determinate before they coloured his last carriage! Alexander quickly rushed to the train window, popped his head in and called,

"Determinate! Determinate, it's me, Alexander! I'm back! I'm alive!" simultaneously looking around to see if anyone heard, which could put them both in danger.

Determinate had never felt so much joy in weeks.

"Boy! You are alive!"

"Yes! Yes! I'm alive! And have lots to tell you. When I couldn't see you, I thought you had left me here and gone back home!"

"I would never leave without you! Never! We are bonded here together for a reason. All things are connected."

Alexander told him all that had happened in the mountain, and the transformation that took place.

"Did you work out a plan to get back home?" he asked the train. "What was it like here for you? What are they doing to you? What are they doing to the people here? I want to know it all. Tell me."

"They modified me inside and out, as you can see. They upgraded my system but I managed to block them from gaining entry to my personal processing unit. They are working hard, night and day, by driving me up and down, to find the light vortex where we appeared on the track. I have a great idea of where it might be. I feel a very strong energy like I'm in the midst of a magnetic field, only at just one particular location on the track. And I could feel the direction of force pulling to that side. But they can't feel it. It seems like I'm a trigger and a key to generating the vortex, I don't know how." Determinate started to whisper and Alexander leaned closer to hear. "I decided to close my processor down until we can find a way to escape but I need to try my hypotheses first to see if it's open before we attempt to escape."

"My time is up. I must go. I can hear them coming," said Alexander, standing up straight.

"Go! Quickly! See you within the next fortnight. Alexander! Wait! One more thing," said Determinate, "I heard the people here saying that they are holding prisoners on the island called Kilard. Only the trains that can transform into aeroplanes can get to that island as there are only landing tracts and no runaways, and they are killing men, women, and children here who dare to stand against them."

"Thanks for the information," replied Alexander. "That's one of the reasons why the elders sent me on this trip, to find out where they are keeping the leader prisoner."

Then he ran towards the farmers, who were getting ready to go back to the mountain.

Before leaving the city gate, Alexander and the others were searched, pushed and pulled by their guards. In fact, the guards kept a close eye on them all the way. The worse thing Alexander feared was that they could be right beside them, invisible, and they would not notice until the creatures struck. The rule was always to be very quiet coming back at least until they no longer had sight of the city gate. As the wagon got to the last checkpoint at the foot of the mountain, while the creatures were searching, Alexander noticed that they wouldn't touch the necklace. Moreover, they moved away from it multiple times when it swayed at their hands as they tried to search him. Yet again this was something to keep quiet about until he was sure what was going on or until he could fully trust someone.

The scene was overlooked by the evening sky. Alexander realised that it never really got dark here. It seemed like there were no nights. All the different lights from the nearby planets made the sky look more like the northern lights in Alexander's world. It was breathtaking to see and Alexander couldn't overlook the glorious view of the setting of the sun from the western side of the hill. It was like watching the sunsets at the Ricks Cafe in Negril.

***

Rebecca had just given the information to Mary.

"Thanks, Rebecca," Mary said.

"You are welcome. I hope this information will help you. However, there are some names I couldn't find on our database. Try and check the hospital record, free information section. There should be records of the doctor they are registered to or of their birth parents."

The little investigation team gathered around the study table, joined by Garcia, Alvin's ex-military friend, looking at all the names, pictures and information just given by Rebecca.

"Let's group them by family last name and gender," suggested Garcia.

After a few hours of going through the data, the team recognised that some of the names could not be traced back further than 70 years, looking at grand and great-grandparents. They separated those and cross-referenced them with their list of the names of suspected people.

"OK, let's see," said Garcia. "We have identified five possible suspects; this has given us new intelligence and a perfect place to start. These selected individuals have no names or any known family connections to this village. Frustratingly, we are wedged in a corner and don't know what to do or where to look for help next."

Frustration definitely appeared on the faces around the table. Hitting a brick wall and sensing their road had come to an end. Not nice.

"What can you do, Garcia?" asked Alvin cautiously.

"I will make a call to a Captain. He owes me a favour. He is still serving and has a higher clearance level that he can use to access additional information. He is known as being one of the government's best at what he does."

Without waiting for the team's response, Garcia made the call immediately and put the phone on speaker so everyone could hear.

A sharp manly voice answered briskly, "Maxwell Brown."

With no small talk required, all five names were given to the Captain who quickly researched them in his system and reported back,

"Four of the names indicate that they migrated here from other parts of the world, with strong family connections and evidence of birth."

The team was not particularly happy with the Captain's findings so far. However, he progressed and revealed something they did not expect. The fifth name did not come back on a global database and with no long line of family tree or birth parents. It looked like he had just appeared over the last 100 years and changed names twice. Now, THAT sounded promising. And the fifth name was… The Chief of Police in their village.

"Wow. The fact that your Chief of Police can't be traced, this seems to be getting more and more serious," Garcia said.

"Oh. My. God," Little Johnny excitedly gasped.

"This is becoming bigger than us here, this has escalated so quickly and puts us in danger," said Alvin, beginning to worry.

"In what way?" Little Johnny asked.

"He may have all the security intelligence and power to be alerted when anyone runs a search on him," replied Garcia.

"What should we do?" asked Mary. "By the looks of it, we would need to carefully track his whereabouts every day and night."

"Leave this to me, this can be dangerous," said Garcia, accepting the challenge.

***

Alexander finally arrived back at the mountain and was sitting in his favourite place looking at the colourful sky when he was unexpectedly called to the combat training area. It was time to start training in peace and wartime combat. This training was nothing compared to that of his world and was nothing like he had seen on TV or on his gaming console. The weapons here were powered and formed out of materials from the asteroid that fell from the sky.

There were other energy sources here, apart from the 10 common types known in Alexander's world. He remembered his science teacher explaining that energy cannot be created or destroyed, it can only be transferred from one form to another. In this world, there was another energy, called the super energy. It could be used to destroy any other energy force. This different type of energy force could only be controlled by one's mind. Whatever your eye saw and whatever your mind thought, could happen. But only the chosen one could be trained to use that power.

The progression of Alexander's training brought into question whether the energy was controlling him, or the other way around. Alexander could hear people's thoughts before they voiced them. After the training was over, there was a mysterious question that plagued Alexander's mind in his world, which he hoped could be explained here by the elders; whether the eggs come first or the chicken. The oldest and the wisest elder explained that in their long line of family history, thousands of years ago, there were no eggs and no chickens, nor any other birds or animals that hatch from an egg.

The elder lectured, "Our first encounters with eggs weren't until an asteroid crashed here. Not only did this rock come with dust and particles, but with other living organisms and eggs of many sorts. We are still to this date, with all advanced technology, unable to find out which planet this came from. This is difficult, as some planets move around at a much greater speed and cannot be traced easily. Some eggs produce birds and animals for our food, but some hunt us for food. They cover land, air, and sea."

Alexander made another incredible discovery in this world, compared to his. In his world, the rainbow appears as a semi-circle, peaceful, and lovely to see. Here, there were two types of rainbows. The semi-circle, like in his world, but then the second one, which appeared to everyone, took the shape of a full circle. Whenever this one appeared, everybody was on a nervous alert, because it looked like a two-way mirror. The people and the creatures of this world could see all types of evil lurking behind it and trying to come through, but something prevented the evil from piercing an invisible barrier.

They said this rainbow only appeared once a year when there was an eclipse of other solar planets, the sun and their world. The sight of the dangerous magnitude of giant-like creatures looking through the full-circle rainbow indicated that what was on the other side looked much more dangerous than the creatures that had invaded here.

The elder explained to Alexander, "They come to this circle every year looking and waiting as if they know one day the barrier to this world will be broken."

The more he heard, the more he decided that he didn't want to be here when that happened.

"What is keeping this barrier in place?" he asked.

"We have been told that climate change can break down the layers between worlds, by the elders that came before us, but we can't be sure," said the elder. "We have spent years observing the creatures in this world when this full circle rainbow appears, and even they show great fear of what is likely to break through one day. This kind of fear could only mean that they have seen these creatures before and know exactly what they are capable of," he said and shuddered. "One of our elders was badly injured during the invasion. Before he passed away, he told us he had heard the creatures referring to the creatures beyond the rainbow as the 'devil's army'. He heard their leader giving strict instructions for a book that they had stolen to be continuously guarded and it must never be opened. Within that book lies the key for good and evil, the beginning and end of all things. He sadly died before we could know more. Up to this day no one has been able to identify the book they are talking about. So, we kept this a secret from the others."

"The more I learn about this world," thought Alexander, "I am beginning to understand that tomorrow is like an unknown seed that has been planted and no one knows what it will bring."

***

Available worldwide from Amazon

Michael Terence
Publishing

www.mtp.agency

www.facebook.com/mtp.agency

@mtp_agency

Printed in Great Britain
by Amazon

21161509R00079